SERGE BASTARDE

ate my

BAGUETTE

summersdale

SERGE BASTARDE ATE MY BAGUETTE

Copyright © John Dummer 2009

Summersdale Publishers Ltd
46 West Street
Chichester
West Sussex
PO19 1RP
UK

www.summersdale.com

Printed and bound in Great Britain

ISBN: 978-1-84024-770-1

Substantial discounts on bulk quantities of Summersdale books are available to corporations, professional associations and other organisations. For details telephone Summersdale Publishers on (+44-1243-771107), fax (+44-1243-786300) or email (nicky@summersdale.com).

John Dummer

SERGE BASTARDE

ate my

BAGUETTE

ON the ROAD in the REAL RURAL FRANCE

SERGE BASTARDE
BROCANTEUR

CONTENTS

PREFACE

I was beginning to wish I hadn't accepted Serge's kind offer to show me 'the true life of a French *brocanteur*'.

Serge's surname was Bastarde (I'm not making this up). He had 'SERGE BASTARDE – BROCANTEUR' printed in big letters on the side of his van. He was a short, tough, balding bloke with wiry grey hair and a ready wit. When he found out I was English and that I wanted to start up in the antiques trade he had gone out of his way to be helpful and had taken it upon himself to show me the ropes. A *brocanteur* is the French equivalent of a bric-a-brac or antiques dealer in England, and they have a long tradition of buying and selling in the colourful open-air markets all over France. I found Serge's advice mostly useful and it would have been churlish to have refused his invitation to accompany him on a trip out in the country to 'forage for hidden treasures'. If the truth be known I secretly couldn't resist the novelty of passing time with a bloke called Serge Bastarde...

1

PIGS AND PEGS

'Ooooh, look! They're washing their pig!' It was a touching sight, the epitome of simple country folk togetherness. The whole family – mum, dad, grandma, grandpa and all the kids – around a big stone trough in the yard with their sleeves rolled up. We had come bombing down a quiet country back lane in Serge's old Renault van to arrive at a typical farm *mas* – a house and several large stone barns grouped round a cobbled courtyard with a surrounding wall and big wooden gates. And there they all were, having the time of their lives.

I could see the old sow's head and her back over the side of the trough. Pigs must get really dirty plunging about in all that mud and need a good washing now and again. Serge tooted his horn and they turned as one to wave at us, happy smiling faces enjoying their carefree country living. But now, with all their hands in the air, I realised just how mistaken I was. Blood and gore was running down their arms. These people weren't washing their pig at all. The miserable animal had just been slaughtered and they were in the process of disembowelling it.

As we drove through the gates and bumped over the cobblestones I could see a couple of legs and trotters sticking up and a long, livid slit in the carcass.

This was exactly the sort of confrontation with the realities of animal husbandry that had turned me and my wife Helen into vegetarians since moving to France. In fact, as a reformed alcoholic ex-smoker vegetarian who disliked sunbathing, I sometimes wondered what the hell I was doing living in France at all.

The farmer stood up and came towards us with a quizzical smile, followed closely by two of the youngest kids, a little boy of about four and a girl who might have been his twin sister. Their faces were spattered crimson. The farmer lifted his elbow to be shaken to avoid smearing our hands with congealed blood and waited to see what we wanted. Over in a corner by the barn a vicious dog that looked like a cross between a German shepherd and the Tasmanian Devil fought to break free of its chain and devour us.

Serge and I had been touring around all morning, 'cold calling' on the most far-flung farms and cottages. Serge would strike up a conversation with the inhabitants to ask if they had any old furniture or junk they wanted to get rid of. If his question elicited a lukewarm response he would pull out a thick wad of euro notes and wave them temptingly under the householder's nose. So far this technique had yielded a few old chairs, a broken-down kitchen table and a rusty standard lamp. But Serge remained undaunted. Maybe our luck was about to change.

He reached down, ruffled the little girl's hair and beamed his sincerest smile at the farmer. '*Bonjour, m'sieu*. We are carrying out some important work for the commune,' he lied. 'They have asked us to visit all the farms in this vicinity and perform a much-needed service, to pick up any old unwanted furniture and stuff that needs to be got rid of. We have already helped out some of your neighbours.' He waved vaguely towards the van. 'Might you have any old bits and pieces you don't want? Things that are hanging around the house gathering dust that we can take off your hands?' The farmer wiped his hands on his shirt and appeared to be considering the question. The dog had decided we were no threat and stopped barking. The rest of the family carried on with their grisly work. 'We're not here to waste your time – we're honest, professional people. We'll pay you for anything of value.'

The farmer's attention was beginning to wander. He glanced back at his pig in the trough. He didn't want to appear rude. The French habit of *la politesse* is a deeply engrained one. He rubbed his hand across a bristly chin. 'No, nothing like that,' he said. 'I'm sorry, I wish I could help you, but...' Serge flashed me an ironical smile. When he reached in his pocket and pulled out the wad of notes, the effect on the farmer was quite remarkable. All thoughts of sausages, bacon and smoked ham were instantly wiped from his mind. His eyes opened wide, hypnotised by the money. 'Of course, we'll pay you for anything we take... in cash,' said Serge. He fanned the notes in the air.

'What sort of things are you looking for?' asked the farmer. 'I suppose we might have some stuff we don't want.'

'I know,' said Serge. 'Why don't we take a walk round the house? I can point out the sort of thing we'd be interested in and what it's worth. Then you can see if you'd prefer to keep it or take the money.'

The farmer liked this idea. We followed him across the courtyard past the rest of the family, who carried on cheerfully hacking away at the dead pig, piling up a mess of intestines and vital organs on a stone slab.

The farmhouse was cool and shady after the hot sun and it took a moment for my eyes to adjust. We were standing in a typical French farm kitchen running into a sparsely furnished living room. The floor was tiled and, apart from a kitchen table, a few worn easy chairs and a television, there was no clutter to speak of and very few decorations of note: a cheap kitchen clock and the local fireman's calendar pinned to the wall; a palm cross; a small plaster figurine of St Bernadette of Lourdes in an alcove. These were honest, hard-working farming folk. They were out in the fields most of the day. The chances of finding any of the valuable antiques Serge was expecting were slim.

I was beginning to feel like an evil money-grabbing bastard. Serge was acting like his surname and this was the first and last time I intended coming out with him on such a cheapskate mission. Helen and I would stick to buying our *brocante* in the auction rooms in future, even if you did have to pay through the nose for it. At least it left you with a clear conscience. Serge was looking around, unimpressed. 'Sure you haven't got any old furniture or clocks you don't want? We pay quite good money for old bronzes, things like that.'

The old boy shook his head and racked his brains.

'What about upstairs? Any uncomfy old oak beds you don't need?'

I couldn't believe Serge was wasting the bloke's time like this. He'd seen the kids in the yard. This family needed all the spare sleeping accommodation they could muster. I wanted to get out of here and leave these good people to carry on preparing their porky comestibles for the coming winter. They didn't deserve to be bothered by creeps like us. I was about to let Serge know how I felt when the old boy's face lit up. 'We have got some old furniture which we dumped out in the barn a few years back,' he said. 'We needed the room and it was a bit gloomy.'

Serge threw me a meaningful look. 'That's the sort of stuff we're after; gloomy old furniture. You've got it right there, all right. Horrible stuff! That's exactly what the commune told us to pick up and get rid of. Clean up all the old junk, the mayor said.'

'I suppose it could be worth something to someone,' said the farmer as we followed him through the back door to some broken-down outbuildings. 'It's good sturdy stuff... been in my family for as long as I can remember, maybe even before the Revolution, it's that old.'

Serge winked at me behind the farmer's back and rubbed his hands together in glee. There were pigeons roosting in the eaves and the door was hanging off its hinges. When the old boy shouldered it open with a bang, there was an explosion of feathers and a couple of squawking chickens tore through our legs. Inside, the air was thick with floating feathers and powdered chicken excreta. Brilliant shafts of sunlight shone down through the murky fog of dust onto strange, bulky shapes piled up high against one wall. When I drew in a breath I could feel a film of chicken shit forming at the back of my throat.

The farmer made a sweeping gesture. 'Well, there it all is. If you think you might be able to do something with it...'

As the dust began to settle, it was patently obvious that these bulky shapes were not the pieces of priceless furniture we had imagined, but huge piles of sidepieces, backs, cornices, legs, doors and other assorted parts. Some well-meaning individual had reduced this load of 'gloomy old furniture' to easily transportable antique flat packs. Serge stood with a look of horror and disbelief on his face. It was the first time I'd seen him speechless.

'There's a whole houseful of old-fashioned stuff there,' said the farmer, carrying on oblivious. 'Buffets, cupboards, beds, dressers, armoires – you name it.'

'Who did this?' Serge was trying to control himself, but his voice had a hysterical edge to it. 'Tell me, my good man, why exactly is this furniture in pieces?'

'They were so big we couldn't get most of them through the doors,' said the farmer, unfazed. 'Me and my son knocked out all the little wooden pegs and dismantled them. Don't worry, every bit is still there. We've even got all the little pegs in a bag somewhere; I'm sure I can find them for you.'

Serge was trying to come to terms with the shock he was experiencing, gazing up at the piles in disbelief. He pulled the edge of a door that was sticking out and it wobbled precariously, threatening to topple down on him. Stepping back, he eyed it apprehensively. 'I suppose if all the bits are there we can put them back together again.'

He was reassessing the situation. He began to examine sections in a smaller pile, one by one, turning them over to see if he could work out what they were exactly, throwing up clouds of dust as he pulled them about. 'I'll just go and clean myself up a bit,' said the old boy, examining his bloodied hands. 'You can think about what you want to do.'

He went back out into the yard and there was the sound of a tap running and water sluicing about. Serge wiped sweat and dust from out of his eyes. 'OK, when I first saw this pile of junk I was disappointed. But look here...' he pulled at a heavy walnut door. 'This is the front of a Louis XV armoire. If the rest of it's here, like the old boy says, then we can reassemble it, oil it up and give it a few coats of wax. No one will ever know. Some of this stuff is eighteenth-century. There are loads of doors, cornices and legs. There could be as many as five or six armoires here. I could sell each one for about fifteen thousand francs [roughly £1,500 – Serge still did all his calculations in francs despite the introduction of the euro]. So you don't need to be much of a mathematician to calculate that there's a small fortune's worth here.'

The reality of what he had stumbled on was beginning to get through. 'This can't be it, can it, Johnny, the moment I've dreamed of, the day God smiles on me and makes me a rich man?'

I didn't have a chance to answer him. The farmer had returned and was standing in the doorway waiting for our verdict with an expectant look on his face. 'Well, yes, this could be of some use, I suppose,' said Serge, instantly changing his deportment to one of pessimistic disinterest. 'But it's all a bit far gone, to be truthful. I'm not sure what we could do with it. We might end up burning most of it.'

The farmer held out a small cloth bag. 'Here are the pegs,' he said. 'I knew I had them somewhere.'

'Me and my colleague here, we'll shift all this junk ourselves,' said Serge. 'Load it up and get it off your property today for no charge whatsoever. How does that sound?'

The farmer looked disappointed. 'OK. Look.' Serge pulled out the wad of notes and peeled off some twenties. 'Take this... one hundred euros. That should about cover it.'

The farmer didn't move. 'A lot of this furniture has got sentimental value to me and my family. I grew up with it. It's like old friends in a way.'

'All right then, to save any argument…' Serge peeled off four fifties. 'Here, take this – two hundred euros, and that's my final offer. It's not worth us bothering for any more than that.'

The farmer's face went blank. He shuffled his feet and looked back outside to where his pig was waiting. I picked up from him a strong impression that we had outstayed our welcome.

Serge looked irritated. 'All right, I'm not an unreasonable man. So how much do you want for it, bearing in mind that it's all in bits?'

The farmer turned back to us, deadpan. 'I couldn't take less than one thousand euros.'

Serge looked like he'd been slapped in the face. 'One thousand euros!' He attempted a mocking laugh but it stuck in his throat and came out more like a cry of pain. He turned to me with a theatrical expression of disbelief, as if asking me to verify how ludicrous it was. His face was white, drained of all blood. I could sense a mixture of battling emotions, as his habitual tightness fought against his greed to possess this potential goldmine of highly desirable furniture. Finally the greed won. He began to peel off a string of fifties. 'OK, let's not quibble about this. Call it five hundred and you've got yourself a deal.'

The farmer put his hands behind his back. 'A thousand or nothing. My ancestors scrimped and saved to buy all this. I'd be betraying the traditions of my family if I took less.'

Serge was flabbergasted: he clearly had not expected this sort of resistance. Teetering on the edge, he was unwilling to concede but tempted by the huge profit he hoped to make. The end was inevitable. He caved in.

'All right, but against my better judgement.' He looked sick. 'Here you go then, one thousand.' He grimaced as he slapped the last few notes into the farmer's hand. The old boy carefully recounted the money and then folded it up into a wad and placed it in his shirt top pocket.

'You'll have to excuse me, but...'

'You need to get back to your pig, I know,' said Serge.

The farmer smiled and tapped his top pocket. He gave me a wink and went out, leaving us to it. Serge was in a state of shock.

'Did I just hand over a wad of money to that old peasant?' He shook his head as if trying to clear his brain. 'For God's sake don't tell anyone about this. I must be losing my touch.'

'But you reckoned this stuff is worth a fortune,' I reminded him. 'Surely your conscience will be clearer now you've paid a fairer price.'

'Conscience? What's that got to do with it? Conscience? This is business. And besides, I don't think I've got a conscience, or not that I ever noticed.'

He pocketed what was left of his money and I followed him out to fetch the van. We pulled it round the front of the barn and began to load up. Some of the pieces of furniture were so heavy we puffed and blew as we staggered under their weight. I could see now why the farmer and his son had knocked them to bits. In their original form they would have been virtually impossible to shift.

The van was soon full and groaning under the burden of the heavy oak and walnut sides and doors. We drove to

Serge's place, unloaded it and stopped for a quick lunch. When we got back to the farm the family were nowhere to be seen. Most of the pig had vanished. There was just the head, the neck and a couple of haunches left in the trough. All the innards had gone, no doubt salted away for further preparation. The dog had disappeared as well. His chain hung empty from the barn wall. I prayed his slavering jaws were chewing on a tasty piece of piggy somewhere and he'd be too preoccupied to spring out and bite us.

The dust had settled in the tumbledown outbuilding and although the remaining pile of furniture still looked pretty daunting, the end was in sight. 'Another van load should do it,' said Serge, spitting on his hands.

We sorted through the remaining oak boards and pieces and I kept a weather eye out for the German shepherd. I couldn't imagine the farmer letting a dangerous dog loose to roam about, but I wasn't entirely convinced. There was a fruitwood door with worn brass hinges leaning against the wall. This lifted Serge's spirits somewhat. He reckoned it was part of an eighteenth-century buffet that, once reassembled, could be worth at least double what he'd paid out.

When we lifted it up to pack it in the van, I noticed an oval opening in the wall with a crumbling brick surround and rusting iron bars. It appeared to be some sort of cellar and I got a shock when something moved deep down in the darkness. For one terrible moment I thought this might be where the dog was kept when he wasn't out on the chain frightening people. But then two hands grasped the bars and a face materialised. It was wild and grubby, framed in a shock of dark curly hair. Two brown eyes looked into mine. I blinked, and the face was gone.

2

POLICE AND PRISONERS

'Come on, let's get this last lot finished and we can call it a day.' Serge had come back in from loading. I pointed at the hole in the wall.

'Yes, yes, it's a cattle window,' he said, matter-of-factly. 'The peasants probably kept a few cows down there separated from the goats or whatever up here – the window was there so they could munch away at the straw through the bars.'

'There's someone in there.' He looked at me as if he hadn't understood. 'I saw someone... a face.'

Serge grinned at me as if I was joking about. 'It's probably one of the kids playing down there. Come on.' He grasped a heavy oak board. 'Grab the other end of this and we'll press on. We haven't got all day.'

I ignored him, bending down close to the bars and peering through. 'Believe me, it's nothing,' he said. 'You're seeing things, my friend.'

I picked up the board with him and we plonked it in the back of the van. But I couldn't stop thinking about the face. I hurried back inside just in time to catch the twinkle of a pair of eyes and see two hands slip away from the bars again. Serge, who was close behind me, had seen them too. 'Do you know what, I think you may be right. How very strange.'

We made a circuit of the barn and discovered a heavily bolted locked door on the far side. 'This is a bit unusual,' said Serge. 'I've never known outbuildings locked like this unless there's a dangerous animal inside. Look, it's really none of our business. I'm sure there's some perfectly sensible explanation. Let's just finish loading up and get out of here.'

'How can you say that? If someone is shut in down there they need our help. We can't ignore this.'

'Just watch me,' said Serge. 'Listen, British, strange things go on in the country. If we took notice of every odd thing we came across, we'd never get anything done.'

He led the way back into the barn and began to sort through the pieces. I couldn't take my eyes off the barred window. As we lifted another heavy section of furniture the face reappeared. We both stood straining but unable to move, fascinated. There was no mistaking the fear in the eyes. I looked at Serge and we slowly lowered the piece. When I looked back the face had gone. Serge shook his head and we carried on. We managed to get all the rest of the bits in the van. Serge slammed the back doors shut. 'We've got to do something about that poor devil,' I said. 'I couldn't live with myself otherwise.'

'I'm not sure we should interfere,' said Serge. 'Let's just forget the whole thing.'

'Someone's shut in down there,' I said. 'I'm going to get him out and if you're not prepared to help me, that's just too bad.'

I went round to the locked door and after a short search managed to find a key hanging from a length of baler twine on a rusty nail in one of the beams. When I tried it in the padlock it opened with a click. Serge had joined me. His curiosity had overridden his desire to make a quick getaway. We shot back the bolt, pulled open the heavy barn door and peered in. It was dark as a wolf's mouth in there. Just a soft glow of light from the barred window. Serge stepped over the threshold. 'Hello, it's only us. Come out, we won't hurt you.'

Considering whoever was in there hadn't the faintest idea who we were, I doubted very much they'd be reassured. We stood listening, peering into the darkness. Finally, Serge lost patience. 'See, there's no one there. It was just one of the kids.'

As he went to pull the barn door shut, there was a sudden rustle in the straw, a thump against the wood and a figure burst out, pushing past, almost knocking us over. It zigzagged across the yard, crouching low, hair bouncing round its shoulders leaving in its wake a distinctive whiff of unwashed body odour. We watched it leap a gate into a nearby field, run up towards some woodland and disappear from sight.

We stood stunned. The only sound was the gentle cooing of pigeons in the rafters. 'Rude bugger,' said Serge. 'Not much of a conversationalist. I warned you not to interfere, Johnny.'

'We ought to talk to the farmer,' I said. 'Find out what's going on. Why would anyone be locked in a barn like that?'

'Like I said, it's none of our business,' said Serge.

We got back in the van and drove across the deserted yard and out through the gates. 'I think we should let someone know about what's happened,' I said. 'Maybe call in at the nearest *gendarmerie* and tell them what we saw.'

'You must be mad,' said Serge, shuddering. 'We never go to the gendarmes about anything... ever! Believe me, it's asking for trouble.'

We had entered the main street of the nearest village and a 'GENDARMERIE' sign came into view. 'Pull up outside,' I said. 'I'm going to report it.'

'I honestly don't think we should. It's madness to put your head above the parapet and draw attention to yourself.'

'Look, there's been some poor devil been kept prisoner in a barn for God knows how long and now he's running free, half out of his mind. We ought to let the authorities know so they can do something about it.'

Serge pulled into the kerb and turned off the engine. 'All right, if you put it like that. But don't forget who let him out. Be careful what you say. Some gendarmes can be right buggers.'

We went through the iron gate, up a concrete path and stopped at the varnished wooden door. Serge looked scared. 'And don't forget to call them all *m'sieu*.' He pulled a face. 'They like that.'

I pushed open the door and we went in. Inside was an open-plan office with a long, shiny-topped reception desk. A fat ginger cat was fast asleep on a pile of books at one end. We stood and waited, watching a young officer in shirtsleeves with cropped hair poring over some papers, marking crosses with a black Bic pen. It looked like he was filling in his lottery entry form. When I coughed he glanced up and slowly rose, marking a couple of final crosses as he did so. He came over with an expectant look on his face, snapping into official policeman mode.

'Sorry to bother you, *m'sieu*,' I said, 'but we felt we ought to report something.' I looked at Serge and he gave me a sheepish smile. 'We were up at a local farm and we discovered something a bit peculiar.'

'Oh, yes,' said the officer. 'What farm was that then?'

I described as closely as I could how to get to the place. He looked mystified, as if he was having difficulty understanding me.

'That accent. You're not from round here?' He said it like an accusation.

'No, he's a *rosbif*,' chipped in Serge. 'From England.' He gave a little hysterical laugh. 'I can barely understand what he's on about myself sometimes.'

The gendarme looked slightly irritated. 'What do you want exactly?'

An older policeman with a big handlebar moustache had come over to see what was going on. He looked formidable, like he was used to taking charge of difficult situations.

'We were up at a local farm buying up some old furniture when we saw something bizarre,' I said. 'We thought we ought to report it.'

'Buying up old furniture?' He sounded surprised.

'Yes, we're *brocanteurs*,' I said. 'We were buying furniture from the farmer. We've got it in our van.'

'Nothing of much value really,' said Serge. 'Just some old bits and pieces.'

The officer looked as if he was carefully contemplating the information. 'I'm assuming you've got all the necessary papers.'

There was an element of threat in his voice.

'Oh, yes, we're professional *brocanteurs*, *m'sieu*,' said Serge, obsequiously.

'Let's see them... the papers.'

He held out his hand, waiting. Serge turned to me. 'Show them your papers then.' His eyes were panicky.

I hurriedly searched through my wallet, found my yellow *carte professionale* and handed it over. The officer examined it closely, studying my face and comparing it with the photo on the card before giving it back. He turned to Serge. 'What about you then?'

Serge looked cornered. 'Oh, I'm just helping him out. I'm not registered at the moment... Taking a break, so to speak.'

So that was why he wanted me to come 'cold calling' with him. The crafty old sod. It was all starting to make sense. Without up-to-date professional papers he was vulnerable.

'But you're a *brocanteur* as well?' said the policeman.

'I am sometimes, but...'

'Only sometimes, is it?'

'When the work's about,' said Serge. He was starting to lose it. 'When it's quiet in the winter I have a rest... you know... spend time at home with the wife and family.' He gave a sickly smile.

'Identity card?' said the officer, grimly.

Serge patted his pockets. He pulled out a filthy grey handkerchief followed by a knotted piece of string and a broken penknife. 'It must be in the van.'

'Let's go see then, shall we?' said the officer as if he was used to listening to a pack of lies.

We trooped out to the van and waited while Serge fished around in the glove compartment. The officer with the moustache was losing his patience. 'All right then, let's see your car papers.'

Serge rummaged around and produced some torn registration documents. Moustache took them gingerly and examined them at arm's length as if they were infected. 'OK, now your insurance details.'

Serge poked around in the front and reappeared empty-handed with a defeated expression. 'I must have left them at home. I'm always worried they'll get stolen.'

He was cornered. The officer was pleased, as if this was the response he was after. 'You'd best fetch them up here then as soon as you like and show them to me if you want to stay out of trouble.'

'I will, *m'sieu*, you have my word on that.'

'It'll be your funeral if you don't,' said Moustache, noting down the van registration. 'Right then, let's see what you've got in the back.'

The two of them stood close behind Serge as he swung back the doors to reveal the dusty pieces of ancient wood stacked to the roof. They peered in, as if this were a trick. Moustache picked up a woodwormy lump and examined it. 'You're *brocanteurs*, you say?' He winked at his colleague. 'Well, that is bits and pieces, just like you said. You've got a bargain here all right.'

The officer with the crew cut sniggered.

'If I were you, I'd burn this lot. We won't detain you any longer. On your way,' commanded Moustache.

Serge went to climb into the van, but I wasn't about to give up so easily. 'There's something strange going on up at that farm,' I said. 'We thought you ought to know.'

They appeared unable to grasp what I was saying. 'We saw someone locked in a barn up there. It sounds unbelievable, but honestly, it's the truth.'

They both looked at each other and then Moustache's face lit up. 'Oh, you mean François?'

'What's he been up to now?' said Crew Cut.

'Poor old François,' said Moustache. 'Best keep him in the dark till he calms down.'

'You mean he's not being held prisoner?' I said.

'Not in the strict sense of the word, no,' said Moustache.

'At least he's up there close to his family,' Crew Cut chipped in.

'But he was locked away in the dark in a cold barn,' I said. 'Surely that can't be right?'

'It's better than having him running around getting up to God knows what sort of mischief,' said Moustache. 'You should have seen what happened last time he was let loose to wander free. We don't want him carted off to hospital again, do we?'

What had we done? I felt like a perfect idiot.

Serge leaned out of the window. 'Come on, Johnny. There's your explanation. Let's go.'

I climbed in beside him reluctantly. 'So, what did he actually get up to last time?' I asked, not really wanting to know but unable to stop myself.

'Best not talk about it,' said Moustache. 'These rumours have a habit of spreading and then where would we be, eh?' He rapped on the van roof. 'And don't forget those insurance papers, you,' he said to Serge.

As we drove off I could see them both grinning happily. We had proved to be an amusing diversion to an otherwise boring afternoon.

Serge was fuming. 'See, I told you, never go to the gendarmes about anything... ever.'

'But how can they know about someone being held prisoner and condone it like that?' I said. 'It's like something out of the Middle Ages.'

'It's nothing to do with us, like I told you, but you wouldn't listen. Now just look at all the trouble I'm in. How am I going to sort out insurance papers in time?'

We drove along in silence. After a bit I said, 'I didn't know you were resting, taking time off to be with your wife and family. In fact, I didn't even know you had a wife and family.'

'Yes, well sometimes you have to tell those sons of bitches what they want to hear. We got off lightly there. Maybe next time you'll listen to what I say.'

We arrived at his apartment and unloaded the stuff into the ground-floor garage. I left him to it, trying to sort out which bit went with which, puzzling over how to put them together. But as I drove home I couldn't stop thinking about old François. What sort of mischief was he getting up to now? He could have been a crazed psychotic killer as far as I knew. What had we done?

Serge phoned me early the next morning, sounding desperate. 'I'm having a bit of trouble here, *rosbif*. You don't think you could come over and give me a hand, do you?'

I turned up to find him in the garage with all the pieces of furniture stacked round the walls. He was in the middle of reassembling a giant wardrobe. He had the back and two sides slotted in the base and was attempting to fix a door into place. They whole edifice was swaying alarmingly as he whacked at it with a hammer, attempting to secure it with one of the little pegs. I rushed to help him, too late, as the heavy wooden back broke loose from the sides and fell forward in slow motion, crashing through the door. Serge leaped back to avoid being crushed but the door caught him and knocked him on his back, pinning him to the concrete floor.

He was cursing freely as I helped him out from under it. 'See this, Johnny? This is what I'm stuck with. I'll never, ever buy anything from a peasant again. You always end up getting conned. They pretend they're thick and lull you into a false sense of security.'

His face was red and sweaty and grimy with dust. 'But what about all this stuff?' I said. 'All the priceless pieces of furniture?'

'Huh! I've been working away most of the night trying to match up the bits, but if there's a complete piece in there I've yet to find it. This wardrobe is the closest I've come and I still can't get the damn thing to hold together.' He looked like he was about to burst into tears. He pulled out a grubby handkerchief and blew his nose. 'Come on, I deserve a rest. Fancy a spot of breakfast?'

I followed him up some back stairs into the apartment, through a gloomy hall, negotiating our way round pieces of old furniture and bits of bric-a-brac, and into a little kitchen at the back which smelled strongly of garlic, onions and damp dog. Serge sat me down at the kitchen table, set a jug of coffee percolating and produced a bag of *chocolatines*. There was an empty basket with a tartan blanket in a corner by the stove. Serge noticed me looking at it.

'That's where my dear old Danton used to sleep. He only died a month ago and I really miss him. I keep thinking I'll get another dog but somehow I can't face it. I'll never be able to replace my Danton.'

I knew exactly how he felt. I had to have our brindle Staffordshire bull terrier, Spike, put down quite recently and just thinking about him still made me well up. Some dogs are irreplaceable and become so much a part of your everyday life that they leave an enormous hole when they're gone.

We ate our breakfast with an air of melancholy hanging over us. We were on our second cup of coffee before Serge unexpectedly perked up.

'Listen, Johnny. Fancy another trip out in the country next week? Who knows what valuable pieces we might unearth.'

I wanted to say no, turn down the offer flat and tell him to find some other mug. But I felt sorry for him.

'OK, Serge,' I said, 'if you're sure it's going to be worth it.'

He was beaming. 'Oh, it'll be worth it all right. Trust me. It'll be worth it.'

3

THE HONEYMOON IS OVER

When I told my wife Helen about what had happened, her response was: 'Typical! I told you not to hang out with that Serge Bastarde. He hasn't a clue what he's doing.'

She'd only met him once, and briefly at that. From past experience I have to admit she's a better judge of character than I am. But even so I thought she was being a trifle harsh. Serge wasn't that bad. And after all, he'd been a *brocanteur* all his life and we were just starting up. In my naivety I was sure I could pick up a few tips from him. Also, he had a lot of local contacts. The prices in auction were almost too high to make a profit; Serge would hopefully put some house clearances our way. Then we could get hold of saleable stuff at a reasonable price.

It wasn't as if Helen and I were a pair of starry-eyed New Settlers. We had originally moved to France on a whim in the late eighties. I had been a drummer with my own blues band in the sixties and later worked as a press officer and 'plugger' in the music business for various record labels. At the onset of the punk era I had joined the embryo doo-wop group Darts, and met and fell in love with Helen when she was a professional photographer doing the first photo shoot for the band. She was an attractive, charismatic redhead with attitude and a great sense of humour. I was completely smitten. My first marriage had disintegrated, my personal life was a mess and I was an infamous character banned from most of the pubs round Clapham for spitting beer and singing dirty songs.

Meeting Helen turned my life around. At first she had no idea I had a drink problem. One of our early breaks with Darts was the group being featured in a Carling Black Label TV advert. We were filmed singing and playing and I was chosen to deliver the punchline 'That went down well!' as we swigged cool glasses of lager after a hot and sweaty gig. We needed several takes to get it right and I put away pint after pint of the stuff. That night, with my head down the toilet, I swore that not another drop would ever pass my lips. I was ready to climb on the wagon. If the Salvation Army had been around I would have signed the Pledge. I was tired of hangovers and sick of being a 'piss artist'. I contacted our local branch of Alcoholics Anonymous and they gave me a 'minder' to give me support. I met him at his flat nearby and was taken aback to find he was an owl fanatic. His place was stuffed with owls. Everywhere were figurines of owls of all shapes and sizes. The walls were covered with pictures of owls. He had owl drinking glasses. Even his bedspread had an owl motif. It was the weird wake-up call I needed.

Soon afterwards, with Helen's help, I managed to totally give up drinking. But that tag line from the Carling Black Label advert continued to haunt me for years afterwards. People would shout out across the street 'That went down well!' and laugh uproariously.

After Darts, Helen and I formed our own group, True Life Confessions, and I went on to manage the seminal three-piece pre-grunge group The Screaming Blue Messiahs. Three years of that and I was starting to feel burnt out and growing disenchanted with the music business from all the craziness of touring Europe and the States.

Helen, meanwhile, had become interested in antiques and had taken to buying in the auction rooms. She started selling at antiques fairs and when I wasn't on tour I began helping out. To my surprise, I enjoyed myself. We went to evening classes together to learn about furniture restoration and I decided, given the choice, I'd rather do this. So I carefully manoeuvred my way out of management and embraced the world of antiques. We had earlier moved out of London to a house in the country in East Sussex near Battle, but now we came up with the idea of living in Cornwall, a place where we had both passed magical holidays as kids. While viewing houses with an estate agent we casually picked up a leaflet advertising properties for sale in France. We took one look at the photos and did a double take at the prices.

The following weekend found us in the Dordogne (where else?), being driven round at breakneck speeds by a roguish French estate agent built like a tubby teddy bear who turned out to be an obsessive womaniser with a string of mistresses. This was 1988 and the invasion of France by the Brits had barely begun. We were enthralled by the Dordogne. It seemed to be aglow with an exotic other-worldly charm. The landscape enchanted us; the prehistoric scarps, wooded hills and walnut trees. We realised how jaded we had become with our life in England.

In the end, we bought an ancient monastery built in a hidden valley. It had huge wooden gates with bronze dragons suspended over it on chains and an enclosed courtyard you might expect to find in a vampire's castle. That had been an exciting time. The novelty of a warm sunny climate; the change of language and lifestyle. A couple of years later we sold up and bought a windmill on a hill in the Alentejo region of Portugal. But eventually, after another two years, unable to speak Portuguese fluently or find work, we decided to return to France at the end of the nineties.

Now the honeymoon period was well and truly over. We had hardly spared a thought for the future and at long last we were having to face up to the reality of surviving in a foreign country when our capital had dwindled to virtually nothing. We still had our interest in antiques, though, and found that as *brocanteurs* we could hopefully earn an income and thereby enter the French system and be covered under their excellent health scheme.

South of Bordeaux along the west coast of France stretch the pine forests of the Landes. But go inland for a few kilometres and you come to the rolling hills and lush green farmlands of a little-known region called the Chalosse. It was here we found a 300-year-old peasant's cottage that was only just habitable and which we bought outright. I set about the restoration with a vengeance but ran out of enthusiasm after rewiring, plumbing and roofing it. We still had a bath in the kitchen, only one finished bedroom and a lone toilet out in the barn adjoining the house.

However, it was luxury after the dilapidated house and windmill in Portugal, where we had to shit in the woods, there was no electricity and our water was pumped up by solar power from a well out back. Besides, a bath in the kitchen is matey and practical. You can chat and drink tea while you soak to your heart's content. I found myself falling in love with this old Landaise farmhouse. It had a strange haunted atmosphere that was difficult to pin down. One of its three barns had been a dairy and there were various giant pieces of iron farming equipment rusting about the place. From our back door we could look over hazy fields stretching out to the nearest little village two kilometres away. But in the summer the maize that our local farmer planted all around us grew high and hid us completely from the outside world until it was cut and harvested. It was an aspect which changed charmingly through the season.

'I promised Serge I'd go out with him again next week,' I said.

'Oh no, you haven't, have you?' There was a note of disquiet in Helen's voice.

'Just for a morning. You never know, we might pick up something worthwhile and we could do with some extra cash.'

Helen looked decidedly unimpressed. She had started having severe bouts of homesickness, missing her brother and her friends in England. Sometimes she suggested we should move back, but when push came to shove we couldn't make a decision. As far as I was concerned I'd have been pleased to spend the rest of my days here and be buried alongside Spike under the apple and peach trees in the orchard.

Travelling about doing *brocante* markets suited me fine. It had many of the qualities I enjoyed from touring with a group as a professional musician. I spent a fair bit of time on the road, and as I got to know more and more of the *brocanteurs* it was like belonging to a big touring club, meeting up in towns and villages. Back in England I hadn't experienced the same sense of camaraderie as I found here in France. Maybe it was something to do with the weather or the French attitude to life. Either way, it didn't feel like work at all.

I remember vividly my first market here. I turned up early at our local *brocante* at Dax, our nearest town, held once a month in the covered market square. Dax is no stranger to us English. The city experienced three centuries of English rule (1152–1453) and Richard the Lionheart is believed to have built the original castle and fortified wall, long since demolished.

As it was my first time out I didn't have a regular place and was obliged to hang around with the *itinérants* (dealers who travel around from market to market, usually *gitans* or Manouche gypsies) until the *placier* (market manager) arrived at eight in the morning to allocate the limited number of spare pitches. I passed the time strolling around, checking out the wide range of bric-a-brac and genuine pieces of French furniture and *objets d'art* for sale.

Under a pile of books on one stall I noticed, with some surprise, an English book – a *Monster Rupert*, one of the original old black and white albums written and illustrated by the creator, Mary Tourtel, and in excellent condition.

I picked it up and examined it to discover it contained one of my favourite stories, 'Rupert and the Magic Hat'. I could scarcely believe my luck. I had this very same book when I was a kid. Its mysterious magic is etched deep down in my psyche somewhere.

The stallholder noticed me reading it. 'Rupert the Bear, eh?' he said in French. 'I prefer Babar the Elephant.'

'Yes, but I had this one when I was a boy,' I told him. 'Bizarre to find a copy here in France.'

'You're English, a *rosbif*, I imagine?' He smiled to himself. He found it amusing for some reason. 'I don't often get foreign books like that. Listen, it's yours if you want it. Why not?'

I looked inside the cover. The price was marked in pencil, fifteen euros, not expensive.

'You on holiday or what?' he asked.

'I'm waiting to get on the market. I'm a *brocanteur*.'

He looked genuinely taken aback. 'Well, good luck to you, *mon ami*.' He held out his hand. 'My name's Serge.' We shook hands and I told him my name was John.

'Look, Johnny, give me ten euros and it's yours. If this book can give you back a piece of your childhood then who am I to stand in your way?'

I was reaching for the money when he stopped me. 'Perhaps you should get over there – that's the *placier* if I'm not very much mistaken.'

I looked across to see the *itinérants* crowding around in a bunch.

'Don't worry, I'll keep the book for you,' he said. 'Pay me later. But if you don't get a move on you won't be working the market today. There aren't many spare places.'

I thanked him and hurried across to tag along behind the straggling *itinérants*. The *placier* was searching for an empty place. When he found one he ran his eyes over us, deciding who should have it. He had a world-weary expression, as if he couldn't wait to get the job over with. One by one our little band diminished until just a handful remained, tagging along behind. It reminded me of waiting to be picked for a team at school, knowing you're about to be left with the losers and 'no hopers'.

We moved up the last aisle and drew level with Serge's stall. There was an empty space right next to his. Serge came over, oozing charm, greeting the *placier* and shaking his hand. He pulled him to one side and chatted quietly to him, nodding in my direction. The *placier* beckoned me over. '*M'sieu* Bastarde says you are a friend of his. You can have this place next to him if you want.'

He turned to the rest of them. 'That's it, no more pitches left,' he said, then shrugged and walked off, clearly pleased to have got the chore over with. The remainder stood shocked for a moment, and then began to drift off muttering, disappointed.

'Better park over there, Johnny,' said Serge. He had placed two wooden chairs on the road to keep anyone from taking my place. I fetched my van from the other side of the square and began unloading my gear. If it wasn't for Serge I'd have been on my way home now. It was then I first saw his white van with SERGE BASTARDE – BROCANTEUR on the side.

He noticed me smiling to myself. 'What's up, Johnny? Anything wrong?'

'Not at all,' I said. 'Thanks for helping me out.'

'It was nothing,' he said. He handed me the *Monster Rupert* book.

'Don't forget this, heh?'

It was strange, but since then I seemed to be spending more and more time in Serge's company. It would be nice to spend more time with our farmer neighbours but the culture differences tend to restrict the subject of conversation. I remember when I was a kid on holiday on a farm in Devon in the fifties trying to describe what a department store was like to the local cowherd boy I'd befriended. He was unable to grasp the concept. The escalators especially, I remember, had him stumped. I'm sure he believed I was making it all up. His life may not have been easier than mine, but it was, on the face of it, less complicated.

The situation out in the country here in France with our farming neighbours is a bit like that. They are honest, warm and friendly folk but you need to find common ground to relate to people, and even though our French is reasonable the differences in our backgrounds often proves to be, if not insurmountable, then at least an unwelcome barrier to the free flow of conversation.

One of our favourite neighbours is a woodcutter and farmer called Roland. In his spare time he plays accordion and sings in a local dance band, which features at fetes and *bals à papa* (old-fashioned traditional dances). He lives with his eighty-year-old mother and has a brace of ex-wives he continues to visit and spoon with. He seems just as loath to let them go as he is to relinquish all the cars he has possessed, which are now rusting in hidden corners of his fields to be lounged in and enjoyed, replete with memories of good times past. In fact, if he isn't using one as a hide to shoot from he is more likely than not entertaining an ex-wife in it.

When he discovered I was a musician he was ecstatic. Did I know 'Ah Wenna', he asked me. I pondered over this. 'Ah Wenna?' I racked my brains. No, I was sorry, but I didn't know that one.

'*Mais oui,*' he insisted. 'The people go crazy for it here. We have to play it several times a night. "Ah Wenna", you must know it.'

Was it a French song by any chance? I asked. How does it go? I gave him the old musician's standby: 'Hum a few bars and I'll soon pick it up.'

He looked exasperated, like he thought I was a complete idiot, cleared his throat and broke into a jazzy rich baritone with a broad accent, the closest English equivalent to which would probably be old Joe Grundy from *The Archers*:

'Ah wenna saints go marching in, ah wenna saints go marching in!'

'Oh – that "Ah Wenna",' I said. 'Of course I know that "Ah Wenna"… Doesn't everybody?'

He grinned happily.

Yes, that's our neighbours. A source of fun, amusement and often good company. And they'll help out if needs be and offer useful advice on any little problem that needs solving. You've only got to ask. But if we try to describe some of the things we've been through in our previous life – the world-weary messed up city one we've turned our backs on – we get a reaction a bit like that cowherd boy. And besides, we'd be embarrassed to let it all out. None of our neighbours went to art school, dabbled with drugs or was an alcoholic hooked on Valium (that was me, all right) or have become so bored or disillusioned with life they upped and took off to another country in search of what? A new beginning? A simpler life? Why had we moved to France? We didn't even know ourselves. After over ten years abroad, any novelty had worn off long ago. We were now facing up to the reality of working and surviving long term.

Maybe that's why I enjoyed Serge's company so much. He instinctively grasped what I was all about. I had to concede, though, that Helen could be right about how much time I was spending with him. While I was out with him, she was slaving away at auctions, trying to buy stuff for us to sell. Without her I'd have been lost.

4

THE LITTLE WOODEN DEVIL

Gerard and Josette are a Gypsy couple, or *gitans* as they are known in France, who drive around in a removal van with a huge Basque flag painted along the side. They quit the wandering life a while back to settle down just outside a small village in the foothills of the Pyrenees where they bought a few hectares of land on which to park a mobile home and keep goats, chickens and a couple of ponies. Gerard is tough and broad-shouldered with unkempt dark hair greying at the temples. He always wears a tracksuit and trainers and walks as if his legs are groaning under the weight of his body. When he smiles, his face lights up to reveal craggy, broken teeth.

I'd seen the pair of them only recently at a regular market held in the little seaside town of Hendaye on the Spanish border. Gerard was sitting on the steps of his lorry under the brilliantly painted Basque flag, looking glum.

'I haven't sold a thing all morning, John. I can't understand it. How are you doing yourself?'

'Middling,' I said. 'Maybe things will pick up this afternoon.'

I couldn't concentrate properly as my eyes were drawn to a little wooden figure on the table, sitting among the Quimper plates and jugs. About twenty centimetres high, hand-carved in walnut, it had an almost medieval quality.

When I picked it up and examined it I could see it was the figure of a miniature devil in a monk's robe. The face was hidden under a cowl, but you could tell it was demonic by the little carved arrowed tail at the back. He was holding a trident in one hand and a small carved book in the other. I turned the little fiend in my hands and examined it more closely. I have an affection for carved wood and I'm also fond of demons in general. Anything vaguely gargoyle or with a gothic flavour attracts me.

'This little chap's interesting,' I said to Gerard. 'How much are you asking for him?'

'Oh, I don't know, John. I picked him up among a load of junk in a house clearance – they sold off the old presbytery in a little village near Bordeaux.'

'Go on, take the horrible little object.' Josette had appeared in the doorway behind Gerard. 'I'll be glad to see the back of the thing. Gives me the creeps, so it does.'

She came round to give me a kiss on both cheeks. I'm always pleased to see Josette. She'd been a real Gypsy beauty once, but the rigours of having a family and life on the road had taken their toll. What she'd lost in looks she'd gained in character and she was still a fascinating woman and a great laugh once she got going.

'No,' I said, 'I'll pay a fair price for him.'

She closed my hand tightly over the little figure.

'Take him. It's a gift. I insist.'

I looked at Gerard. He nodded. 'If you like him, John, you can have him. He cost me nothing. I wouldn't dream of charging you.'

I was touched. It wasn't the first time I'd been surprised by the generosity of a *gitan*. I thanked them and strolled back to my stall with the little figure in my pocket. I sat about after lunch with not much to do, waiting for that elusive sale, but it never came. I was bored and found myself absentmindedly inspecting the little wooden demon.

It was strange, the way the face was concealed under the hood of the robe. There was a chin visible, but the rest of the features were somehow cunningly hidden among the folds. It was an incredibly subtle piece of carving work and clearly executed by an expert. The more I looked to see how the effect was achieved the less I could work out how it was done. I found myself imagining the face under the cowl, and the picture my mind conjured up was not very pleasant...

Later I was holding the figure in my hand, watching to see if a couple of well-heeled customers perusing my stall were about to make a purchase, when I felt it move. It gave me such a shock that I jumped and involuntarily let it fall from my grasp. It bounced off under the table and only after I'd retrieved it on all fours did I manage to convince myself that my imagination had been playing tricks.

I stood it away to one side, but my eyes kept being drawn back to it, picturing the face under the hood. In my mind it began to take on an air of menace. It was no longer simply carved wood, but a creepy little sentient being. I bagged it up and bunged it in a box under the table but I could still see every detail in my mind's eye. And as the afternoon wore on and I'd still sold nothing I began to wish I'd never clapped eyes on the despicable thing. Josette had been right – it was a horrible little object.

In the end I decided to swallow my pride and took it back to tell Gerard I'd changed my mind, he could have it back.

Josette was adamant. 'No, I'm sorry, John, we never want anything to do with it again.'

'Yes, we've sold really well since we got rid of it,' said Gerard. 'If you've gone off it, why don't you put it on your stand and sell it?'

'I wouldn't bother,' said Josette. 'We tried that and everyone was repelled. That's why I was surprised when you said you liked it. You're going to have to give it away like we did. That way you can counteract the hex.'

I was stunned. 'What hex? You mean you gave it to me knowing there was a hex on the foul thing?'

'Well, no, we didn't know exactly,' she said. 'It's just that since it's been gone sales have suddenly picked up. We've come to the conclusion that it must have brought us bad luck. When you're saddled with an unlucky object like that, the only way to be rid of it and break the curse is to find someone who is attracted to it and give it to them. We gypsies know about these things.'

Gerard nodded in solemn agreement. 'Sorry, John, I can't afford the risk.'

'And it's no good throwing it away,' said Josette. 'The hex will stay with you forever then.'

Oh, great! I was going off these two.

'Right, so I'll just have to hang on to him then?'

'Guess so, until you find another mug,' said Josette, breaking into peals of uncontrolled laughter.

'Like me?' I said.

'You said it,' she said, wiping her eyes.

I joined in and laughed with them, and as I packed up my gear later I came to the conclusion that I'd allowed them to spook me. What did they know, superstitious Gypsy folk?

As I was packing up I knocked over a spelter figure of a cavalier whose sword arm broke off when it hit the ground. Then there was a massive thunderstorm as I was loading and most of my stuff got soaked.

On the way home, the sky was ablaze with sheet lightning, and once there was a blinding flash and a deafening clap so close I nearly shat myself. I half expected to see ball lightning rolling past me on the road as I once had years before, driving with Helen. At one point the rain was so heavy I was forced to slow down to a snail's pace as I could barely see the road ahead of me.

The storm eased as I drove down the small winding lane that snakes over the hills near our house and I was thankful to be almost home after a horrendous journey.

Maybe I was so relieved I let my concentration drop (they say most accidents happen within a few kilometres of home), but one minute I was on the road, and the next the van was skidding out of control along the grass verge.

It happened in slow motion and was almost balletic in its grace and simplicity. There was a small sunken stream with steep banks and as the nearside wheels went down the van tipped over onto its side and we glided along gracefully with grass and wild flowers whipping against the window.

I remember thinking, Oh dear, what a nuisance. Looks like I'm going to be late for dinner, and coming to rest hard against the door, looking down at the water gurgling past. I sat for a moment, held firm by my seat belt, thankful I wasn't hurt. Then I released myself and climbed up across the passenger seat, opened the door and clambered out.

It was a beautiful evening. The storm was over and the air smelled fresh and clean, washed by the rain. A blackbird was singing deep in the woodland, a liquid song of joy. The van lay sadly slewed on its side, the stalled engine ticking and gurgling gently as it cooled down. I'd left my mobile at home so set off along the lane to make the short walk home.

When I got there Helen was waiting at the back door, looking worried.

'What's happened? Are you all right?'

There was a note of panic in her voice. I explained.

'I knew something was wrong. I was about to come and look for you.'

This didn't surprise me at all. Helen regularly has psychic premonitions and they're usually correct.

We phoned the *pompiers* (firemen) and they told me to go down and wait by the van. The sun was beginning to sink below the trees when they arrived in the type of square red retrieval lorry I'd seen bombing up the motorway to multiple pile-ups. There were three of them on board: a couple of scruffy assistants in blue overalls and a 'spit and polish' chief with a farcical pointy waxed moustache, shiny black knee-high boots and an immaculate blue uniform. They found the situation amusing for some reason.

'What were you doing, watching the birds?' said the chief. '*Eh alors, vous êtes tombé dans le ruisseau.*'(You've fallen in the stream.)

The hilarity of this escaped me, but I believe there is a French proverb that goes somewhere along the same lines.

One of the assistants rolled his eyes heavenward to indicate that I wasn't to take what the chief said too much to heart. I recognised the chap from our local village. All three of them were unpaid part-timers, supported in the main by donations paid out by locals for the annual *pompiers'* calendar. I always feel obliged to fork out as much as I can possibly afford for my copy, as they keep a list; I imagine our house catching fire and the *pompiers* checking to see how much we've donated towards their calendar before they decide whether to rush to our aid or not. Call me paranoid if you like, but you never know with these things.

The chief got down in the stream, fearlessly wetting his clean boots, and pronounced that we were going to have to drag the van out. This seemed self-evident to me, but I kept my mouth shut.

They attached a tow rope and after much pulling and shoving the van rose gracefully up out of the *ruisseau* back onto the road. There were now a couple of dents in the side panels and I observed that, with its embryo rust spots and battered bodywork, it was beginning to look like every other *brocanteur*'s white van. I also noted when I looked in the mirror at home that I'd grazed my nose in the accident and now looked exactly like Serge Bastarde did some mornings, as if he'd been in the wars. But it could have been worse. At least the van was perfectly serviceable and none of our stock appeared to have been damaged.

I didn't mention the little wooden devil to Helen but as I lay in bed that night I couldn't stop imagining that the fiendish little object was the root cause of my recent bad luck. I was going to have to get rid of it at all costs.

The next morning I was at my local market bright and early to set up my stand. I spent the first half-hour making the rounds, chatting to the other *brocanteurs*, trying to spot if there were any bargains going from recent house clearances. Then I set up my table and sat waiting for the punters to arrive.

As the morning wore on and the market filled up with eager *chineurs* (bargain hunters) everyone seemed to be selling apart from myself. I had placed the little devil in a prominent position on my table, but although a few curious people picked him up and examined him, no one appeared interested in buying, even though I'd ticketed him at a giveaway price.

As lunchtime drew near, I decided to try a psychologically different approach and hid him down behind an art deco clock garniture. Sometimes when people spot an item tucked away out of sight they feel they might be discovering an overlooked bargain. But no one did.

I covered up my wares, strolled over to the local bistro to grab a bite to eat and found Serge in there, propping up the bar, fortifying himself with a glass of Beaujolais and a couple of plates of tapas.

'Eh, Johnny, how's it going? Had a good morning, have you?' He forked in a mouthful of *calmar* (squid) and washed it down with the wine. He had a graze on his nose exactly like mine. We were blood brothers!

'Not too good, no, Serge,' I said. 'I can't understand it.'

'Don't worry, Johnny. It gets like that sometimes. Maybe this afternoon, eh?'

We carried our coffees out and drank them together in the sunshine, watching our tables.

'I don't know why you haven't sold anything, Johnny, you've got some good stuff.'

I watched with trepidation as he picked up an ornate vase and waved it in the air. I shut my eyes and prayed he wouldn't drop it.

Then he spotted the little demon down behind the deco clock and pulled it out.

'What's this then?' He was fascinated. He turned it in his hands, trying to see under the hood and get a glimpse of the face. Eventually he gave up and brought it over.

'This little devil, it's crazy. How much would you sell him for... you know... to a friend like me?'

He was pulling the old pals act so he must have been keen.

'You don't like it do you? Don't you think he's a bit creepy?'

'No, I love him.'

'I thought he might be bringing me bad luck as I haven't sold anything today.'

'Rubbish! I never had you pegged as superstitious, Johnny.'

'You like him... you can have him,' I said, unable to believe my good luck. The little demon must have had the power to attract idiots, like it had me.

Serge looked surprised. 'You'd give it to me, Johnny?'

'Yes, no questions asked.'

He winked at me and his face lit up. 'Oh, I get it, it's like that is it?'

I didn't know what he thought it was like but I agreed and he slipped it into his pocket with a conspiratorial expression on his face.

'Thanks, Johnny. I owe you one.'

'Not at all,' I said. 'Consider it a gift with no strings attached.' I'd have felt rotten about what I was letting him in for if I wasn't so relieved to get rid of the bloody thing. That afternoon my luck began to return and I sold well. I rationalised that it couldn't be anything to do with getting rid of the little devil, but I still wondered guiltily how Serge was doing. He came over as I was packing up, all smiles and bonhomie.

'Hey, Johnny, would you believe it, I didn't sell a thing all afternoon. I was beginning to think you might be right about that little devil bringing bad luck but then DaSilva the Portuguese dealer came along.'

I knew DaSilva. He turned up regularly at the markets and had bought off us before.

'Yes, his eyes nearly popped out his head when he saw the little wooden devil. He said it was Spanish and really old. I had no trouble getting him to cough up three hundred euros for it.'

I couldn't believe what I was hearing. If I'd just hung onto the little devil a couple more hours DaSilva would have bought it from me. The three hundred euros would have been mine. It might have made up for some of the bad luck I'd had. I looked at Serge grinning all over his face. I couldn't help thinking it was a case of 'the Devil takes care of his own'.

He put his arm around my shoulder. 'You're still on for our little expedition though, aren't you, Johnny?'

I thought about what Helen had said about my wasting my time with him. I was about to make an excuse and put him off when he thrust some notes into my hand.

'There, one hundred and fifty euros. You gave that little devil to me, Johnny, so you should have half the profit. It's only fair.'

I was taken aback. I looked at the notes in my hand. I couldn't think straight.

'So, see you first thing Monday morning then?

'OK, Serge,' I said.

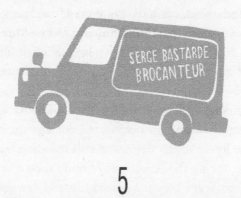

5

GIZZARDS AND BRONZE FIGURINES

The figure was standing stock still in a field in front of the peasant's cottage. As we drew nearer I could see he was an old man dressed in worn overalls and a blue beret. His head turned and followed us as we drove past in the van, and he was still standing, motionless, watching as we disappeared out of sight over the hill.

'Not much point trying that place,' said Serge. 'Looked too poor to bother with.'

We had turned off the main road twenty minutes before and had been winding down little back lanes through woods and over hills past isolated farms and cottages. Against my better judgement I was again accompanying Serge on one of his cold-calling expeditions, hoping to pick up old furniture or bric-a-brac on the cheap. Maybe I could protect the innocent from his greedy, grasping, swindling ways. Fat chance. Who was I kidding?

So far we'd had no luck.

'The bloody peasants have gone mad,' said Serge. 'I blame the television. Now they think any old piece of junk is worth a fortune. Not like the old days when they couldn't wait to get shot of it for peanuts. And of course the car boots haven't helped. Between the two of them they're killing the trade.'

Unexpectedly, the road began to double back on itself until we were coming up behind the cottage we had passed earlier. The figure in the beret was still standing frozen in the same place, facing the direction we had taken a few minutes earlier. When Serge reached across me and pressed the horn the old boy's head zipped round and he almost toppled over with shock. Serge was delighted. He tooted out a greeting and waved.

'Come on, let's try this place.'

'But I thought you said it looked too poor to bother with.'

'Yes, well I've changed my mind. And anyway, what do you suggest? This is the end of the road and it's almost lunchtime. They're dead hospitable, country folk – we might get a free bite to eat.'

Not content just to rip people off, he wanted them to feed him too. I was unfamiliar with French rustic customs but it was past noon and since I'd been living and working in France my stomach had been trained to start rumbling automatically at midday. And we were a long way from any village cafes or shops. Maybe he had a point.

We parked the van and started up the track across the field. The old boy was still watching us as if he couldn't quite believe we were actually about to enter his life. But as we drew level something galvanised him into action. He raised his arm jerkily and set off towards us, hobbling slightly as if his feet pained him. As we waited I found myself drinking in the simple beauty of the surrounding countryside, savouring the tranquillity and the scent of freshly cut grass. This place was about as idyllic as you could get. I knew people back in Britain who would kill to own a little cottage like this one far from the stresses and strains of modern life.

It reminded me of the dream-like period we spent when we first moved out to France. A kind of floating between two worlds. The summer of hazy mornings when the *brume* (mist) swirled up from the River Dordogne to be dispersed by the steaming heat of the afternoon sun. Magical evenings with an unearthly bloated moon hanging low over a landscape that echoed with the constant chirruping of cicadas.

The monastery we had bought was positioned perfectly, standing alone looking over long fields that led to the deciduous woods covering the surrounding hills. You could stand in these fields and hear the sound of rain approaching, hissing in the leaves of the evergreen oaks as it drifted in. It had been so protected there was seldom any wind, just now and then a gentle, balmy breeze. There were wild boar, or *sanglier*, in abundance. On early morning walks we would happen upon herds of them in the clearings. A massive old boar would fearlessly root through our fields. Rutting stags would come down the hillsides bellowing out a challenge.

Our grasp of the language had been so tenuous – rusty, barely used French O level – that when the local farmers pointed out something we didn't understand we passed it off as 'something to do with the war'. Now, from working the markets and hanging out with Serge, I was learning to speak colloquial French like a barrow boy.

The old chap was on the track now and I was slightly taken aback to see that he had no shoes on. His bare feet were nut brown below the frayed bottoms of his overalls. No wonder he was hobbling.

Serge nudged me and waved a welcome, reaching out to grasp the old fellow's hand.

'Good day, sir, good day. What a beautiful day.' He was effusive, pouring on the charm.

The old chap seemed slightly reticent, but perhaps he was overwhelmed by the sheer power of Serge's greeting. When he came to shake my hand his grip was firm and warm, but I felt hard calluses on his palms and fingers.

My heart went out to him. I felt as if we were carriers of some horrible disease about to infect his simple world.

'Sorry to burst in on you like this, Papa,' said Serge cheerily, 'but my colleague and I have been asked to carry out a special survey of the commune by the mayor. He wants us to record who lives where and check out their living accommodation. Simple stuff, really, but vital for the upcoming national census. We just need to take a look around and make a few notes. It won't take long and we don't intend to inconvenience you in any way.'

This was a spiel I hadn't heard before, and the old boy appeared to accept it at face value. It was unbelievable. Mentioning the mayor worked like a charm every time.

'There's only me and my sister here,' he said. 'But come in. Maybe you'd like an aperitif before you begin your work.'

Serge made an 'O' shape with his finger and thumb (his equivalent to the thumbs up) behind the chap's back as we followed him towards the house.

We were ushered into the little cottage which was clean and fresh with a spotless tiled floor and white, lime-washed walls. The old fellow seated us at a table covered with a brilliant yellow plastic cloth and fetched glasses and a bottle from a glass-fronted kitchen cabinet.

Serge nodded at me and beamed as the old boy poured him out a generous helping of Ricard and invited him to add the amount of water he required from a jug. I chose a glass of the strange syrupy strawberry cordial that comes in a metal tubular bottle, and is a popular non-alcoholic drink. It was sickly sweet, but refreshing none the less after a hard, fruitless morning driving about in the van.

The back door was wide open and I could see out into the yard. There was a red rooster strutting about and a few scraggle-necked hens pecking among the pebbles. I sipped at my cordial and was surprised to see a little hunched-over woman duck out from behind a stone shed and scurry across the yard. She looked like a tiny witch with a prominent hooked nose and craggy face. She wore a gloomy robe, with a dark shawl pulled over her shoulders and a scarf tied round her head. She peered through the back door as if trying to get a furtive look at us. And then she was gone, disappearing out of sight behind a barn.

Serge had finished his Ricard. He plonked the empty glass down on the table and sat waiting expectantly for it to be replenished.

'Sorry to bother you at lunchtime like this, but we seem to have got slightly stranded. Do you know anywhere we could get a decent bite to eat?'

The old chap pondered this for a moment. 'There's nowhere really. But my sister would be pleased to cook something for you. You're quite welcome to eat here.'

'That's very kind of you,' said Serge, 'but we don't want to put you to any trouble.'

'It's no trouble at all. It would be our pleasure.'

'Well, if you insist,' said Serge. 'Thank you so much.

The old boy poured himself a second glass of red wine. He knocked back over half of it and his eyes began to twinkle.

'So it's just the two of you live here then?' said Serge.

'That must have been your sister I just saw out in the yard,' I offered.

'She's very shy, not used to meeting many people.' He took another swig of wine. 'She's had a lot to cope with what with one thing and another.'

'Really?' said Serge, disinterestedly. He was scanning the room for valuable furniture or worthwhile bits and pieces.

The farmer was starting to grow garrulous under the influence of the drink and the company. I wanted to stop him. I didn't want him to reveal all the secrets of his personal life to Serge. He might be able to use them against him in some way.

But Serge had his mind on other matters. '*Putain*, that aperitif, it's given me an appetite. When were you thinking of eating?'

'Of course,' said the old chap, 'I'll go and fetch my sister.'

He got up and went out into the yard.

'See, they may be poor,' said Serge, 'but they live like kings, these peasants.' He slapped his rounded belly. 'I'm just about ready for some home-cooked grub.'

The farmer reappeared with the little hunched-over woman bobbing behind him. She began to bustle about in cupboards, head down, barely glancing in our direction. She emptied a clear glass jar full of a yellowy white viscous liquid with grey lumps in it into a heavy iron pan, sprinkled it with herbs and began to fry the lot up on the stove.

Serge rubbed his hands together. 'Mmmm, that smells like *gésiers* if I'm not very much mistaken.' He nodded at me. 'But not much interest to you, eh, Johnny? I don't think you're ready for a nice plate of chicken gizzards just yet.'

He turned to the old boy. 'My friend here is from England where they've got some very strange ways. He refuses to eat meat, would you believe it?'

The farmer looked at me with renewed interest. 'We have some pork if you don't like *gésiers*,' he said kindly. 'We don't meet many English people round here.'

'If you've got any bread and maybe a piece of cheese that would be fine,' I said.

'Estelle, did you hear that?'

The little old woman half-turned and smiled at me before fetching a big country loaf and some Brie which she placed on the table. Then she served up the *gésiers*, which Serge attacked like a ravenous wolf.

'*Putain*, you don't know what you're missing, Johnny. This is delicious.' He poured himself a glass of red wine and washed down a mouthful of gizzards.

The old woman put a pot of coffee on the stove, produced a large cherry flan and cut us each a piece. Serge ate his with gusto, licking his fingers and slurping his coffee. When he'd finished he burped loudly and pulled out his well-thumbed notebook.

'Now, to get things sorted out properly for the survey. It's just you and your sister living here, is it?'

'Yes, just the two of us.'

'And you are *M'sieu...*?'

'Perrier... Jacques Perrier.'

'Ah, yes, and your sister is?'

'Estelle Perrier.'

'Good, good... excellent,' said Serge, scribbling away.

I was beginning to find this pantomime embarrassing and looked away. The little old woman was waiting just outside the door, hiding in the shadows, shyly watching us.

Serge drained his cup of coffee, slammed shut his notebook, stood up and yawned.

'Well, I think that just about concludes our work here. You've been most helpful. Don't worry, I'll mention to the mayor how cooperative you've been.' He shook the farmer's hand. 'We'd better be on our way. Say goodbye to your sister for us won't you, Jacques?'

As we set off along the track towards the van Serge was jubilant.

'There, what did I tell you, Johnny? Who needs to go to restaurants to eat when you've got hospitable peasants like that around?'

But I was beginning to feel upset about how we'd used them.

When I looked back the old man was waving us goodbye. The sad little figure of his sister was standing behind him, framed in the doorway, watching us go.

We drove off with Serge cheerfully humming the popular Serge Gainsbourg hit, 'Sea, Sex and Sun', punctuating the chorus with a series of foul-smelling belches.

'Those *gésiers* were out of this world, Johnny. Beats me how you can pass up on such delicious *bouffe*.'

I was still feeling bad about how I had colluded with him in conning that nice peasant and his sister out of a free meal. I certainly wasn't in the mood to get into any sort of argument with him about eating meat.

We drove along in silence for a while until Serge spotted a sign for a *déchetterie* (a rubbish tip).

'Eh, quick! Turn off here, Johnny. These places can often yield up little treasures.'

We followed a track through the woods to arrive at a fenced-off area where garishly coloured plastic bin receptacles and several heavy metal skips piled high with rubbish stood in a yard strewn with bits of old newspapers and cardboard boxes. There was a wooden hut at the gate with a black and white collie dog tied up with a piece of hairy baler twine outside. It came crawling towards us on its belly with its tail wagging. The hut door was open but there was no one about.

Serge went over to a mountain of old metal and started to pull at a twisted bicycle, threatening to bring down the lot on top of him. I fussed the dog and wondered how far the nearest accident unit was if Serge injured himself.

A man emerged from among the trees, zipping his fly and buckling his belt. He was wearing a badly stained, fringed Western-style shirt, a blue US Cavalry cap and cowboy boots. At a guess I'd have said he'd just had a crap in the woods.

There was a scream of twisting metal and Serge jumped back, narrowly avoiding being crushed, as a big square tank, a heavy iron bath and assorted rusty agricultural machinery came crashing down.

The junkyard cowboy watched as the dust settled and I got the impression that new acquaintances were limited in this particular neck of the woods.

'That's some scrap iron you've got there,' said Serge.

The guy nodded and finished buckling his belt. Serge took him by the hand and shook it.

'We're on the look out for any interesting bits and pieces, discarded bric-a-brac and stuff. We've just been doing a spot of business with old Papa Jacques Perrier up the road and he recommended we pop in here.' Serge was making it up as he went along.

The man nodded to me and began to untie his dog.

'You've been up at Jacques Perrier's place? He doesn't get many visitors these days.'

'He had us round for lunch,' said Serge, smugly. 'His sister cooked for us – fried *gésiers*... Delicious!'

'You saw his sister? How was she?'

'Estelle's fine, just fine,' said Serge, like he was an old family friend.

'That was terrible what happened to her though, wasn't it?' said the man. 'You know, during the war?'

Serge was nonplussed. 'World War Two? You're going back a bit there, mate. I was just a kid.'

'What, you don't know about the family tragedy? I thought everyone knew.'

Serge was starting to get bored.

'No, but you're going to tell us all about it.' He looked at me with a pained expression.

'Her two sons got killed in battle on the same day. It was an awful shock. But that wasn't all – when her husband heard the terrible news he went straight off and hung himself.'

Serge pulled a face like he didn't believe it.

'It's God's honest truth, ask anyone. Estelle found him hanging from a beam in the barn. It finished her off, they reckon.'

The man was relishing the story. He clearly didn't get many visitors here at his tip.

'When she'd buried her husband and her sons all she had left was her brother Jacques. She moved in with him and he's looked after her ever since. In return she washes, cooks and cleans for him... does everything a wife would do for a husband.' He winked at me.

'So have you got anything you might think we'd be interested in or not?' said Serge. He was unmoved by the tale. He predictably pulled out his wad of euros with a flourish from his back pocket.

The man's eyes widened. 'What about that tin bath? That's got to be worth a bit.'

'I'm not after shit,' said Serge rudely. 'Do I look like a *gitan* to you?'

My answer to that question would have been no. Most *gitans* dressed smartly in the latest fashion, unlike Serge, who looked like he'd just tumbled out of bed and pulled on the nearest thing to hand from a pile on the floor. But I was still thinking about poor Estelle. No wonder she hid herself away. Was the wink the man had given me an insinuation that she and her brother were involved in some sort of incestuous relationship? Surely not.

'Hang on a moment, what's that in there?' Serge was peeking through the hut window. 'There, on the desk. That looks like the sort of thing we're after.'

He went in brazenly and came out with a statuette of a naked woman holding a flaming torch with flowing hair covering her breasts and nether regions.

'That's a signed bronze that is,' said the man. 'I found it in a box of rubbish a while back.'

Serge examined it closely. He took out a penknife and scratched the base.

'I'll give you fifty euros for it,' he said finally.

'For a bronze like that? You're mocking me!'

'It's not a bronze; it's a spelter,' said Serge. 'The scratch is dull yellow, not shiny and silvery.'

This was a pathetic attempt at a con. The metal in a spelter figure is a mixture of lead and tin and a small scratch usually shines brightly. Serge knew that if the scratch was dull yellow it was probably a bronze and doubtless the man knew it too.

'I wasn't born yesterday. That statue is definitely a bronze.'

'All right, eighty euros. Take it or leave it.'

The man was tempted. He was pondering the offer. He took off his US Cavalry hat and wiped the sweat from his forehead with the back of his hand.

'Come on, Johnny,' said Serge. 'We're wasting our time here.' He climbed in the van and waited for me to start her up. The man watched us, still clutching the bronze figure. As we pulled away he ran after us, tapping on the window. I stopped and Serge wound it down. The Junkyard Cowboy said, 'OK, look, make it a hundred and you've got yourself a deal.'

'That's more like it,' said Serge. He peeled off a couple of fifties. 'There, you can buy yourself a new Buffalo Billy shirt and *fais la fête* all weekend.'

He took the figurine from him and laid it on the seat.

'You've not got any other old bronzes hidden away in that hut of yours then?'

The Junkyard Cowboy shook his head. He was beginning to think maybe he'd made a mistake.

'OK, Johnny, let's go,' said Serge, winding up the window.

I drove round the pile of scrap iron and out through the gates.

'I know a dealer who'll give me six hundred euros for this little whore, no questions asked,' said Serge as we bumped long the track.

'I've got a good feeling about today, Johnny. A delicious free meal and now this bronze here. Is our luck starting to change or what?'

6

SNOBS

We drove along with the bronze statue bouncing about on the seat between us and Serge shouting out the chorus from a French popular song from the forties. I'd heard it before – a favourite on our local radio station – about a Romeo farmer who can service all his mistresses in the one day thanks to his trusty Mobylette.

He stopped singing. 'Quick! Pull in here. This place looks like it's owned by bourgeois richos with more money than sense.' We were passing a large house with blue painted shutters set back from the road. There was a swimming pool in the garden and a couple of shiny cars parked out front.

I had little faith in Serge's snap judgements but followed instructions and swung into the drive. One of the cars was a four-wheek drive jeep and as we drew nearer I realised it had an English number plate.

'This is no good. It's owned by English people,' I said, braking and starting to reverse out.

'No, carry on, Johnny. I've often bought stuff off the English. They clear out their old junk the same as the French.'

A woman appeared from round the back of the house wearing a floral-print dress and floppy straw hat and carrying a trug and a pair of pruning shears. She came towards us with an expectant look on her face. I felt stupid and wasn't sure how I was going to play this. But she spoke before I had a chance to explain.

'Vous cherchez quelque chose?'

Her French was good. It was obvious she wasn't just someone over for a short stay in a holiday cottage.

I was tempted to answer her in French and pretend we were lost. But Serge was watching me closely and would have noticed I wasn't going through the rigmarole of asking if she had any valuable antiques she was willing to unload on us for a song.

So instead I spoke in English, the first thing that came into my head.

'Sorry to disturb you like this... we seem to have made a mistake and come to the wrong house.'

Serge nodded and grinned as if he knew exactly what I was saying.

He was pleased the woman had spoken French because he chipped in, *'Mais oui, et je peux payer en espèces pour les belles choses.'* (Yes, and I pay in cash for anything good.) He predictably pulled out his wad of euros and wafted them under her nose.

She looked shocked and slightly repulsed.

'Does your friend make a habit of waving his money about?' She had a cut-glass English accent.

'We're on our way to do a house clearance,' I said. 'I'm sorry about that, he never misses an opportunity to try and pick up a bargain.' (I was starting to make up a pack of lies just like Serge. I was turning into him. That was it! I was definitely not coming out with him again.)

'Why, have you got a shop?'

'No, we're *brocanteurs*. We only do the markets,' I said.

'What's the matter, darling?' A man appeared dressed in a pair of brightly coloured swimming shorts and sporting a brilliant white Panama hat.

'These people are knockers,' she said, making it sound like it came just below paedophiles in her list of utter scum.

'Really?' said the man.

'Not knockers, exactly. We're professional *brocanteurs*.' I could feel my face reddening. She reminded me of a particularly scary teacher from my infant school. 'Actually, I've only just started and he's showing me the ropes.'

'But your friend appears to be a knocker. He's certainly vulgar enough with his fistful of money.' She pulled a face as if there was a nasty smell under her nose.

'He's a bit keen but he always pays a fair price,' I lied. It was becoming second nature to me now.

She raised her eyebrows. 'So which is it to be? Are you knockers or are you lost?'

'We're supposed to be picking up some stuff from a house round here… It's for a friend of his,' I said lamely.

I glanced at Serge with his grazed nose and scruffy jeans holding the wad of euros. He had a smear of cherry pie juice on his chin. I wasn't much smarter myself. We looked like just the sort of unsavoury characters these people had come to France to avoid.

'Is he a Gypsy? He looks almost too disreputable to be one.'

'No, he's a Basque,' I said trying to lighten the mood.

'He looks like a common or garden knocker to me. Perhaps he's not the best person to model yourself on if you're hoping to be a legitimate *brocanteur*.

Serge was wondering what we were on about.

'Tell them the mayor sent us,' he said. 'That always does the trick.'

I laughed like this was some sort of joke.

'Yes, well, we'll be off and leave you in peace,' I said, deciding it was best to cut and run. 'Sorry again to have bothered you.' I went to get back in the van.

'Come on, Serge, let's go.'

'Have they got any old English furniture they want to get rid of?' said Serge. 'Save them going up the tip.'

I ignored the remark, laughing it off. 'He's like a little terrier once he scents a bargain.'

I pulled a tight face at Serge. 'No, they haven't got anything. Let's go.'

But he wasn't ready to give up so easily.

He went up to the man, grinning with his hand out.

'The mayor asked us to come round and see you,' he said, immediately calling the man *'tu'* in an overfriendly manner. 'We've visited all your neighbours.'

The man took his hand and shook it. 'Well, that's strange because I *am* the mayor and I've never met you before in my life.' He spoke perfect French.

Serge was completely wrong-footed by this remark.

'No, that's not possible. You can't be the mayor.'

'I can assure you I am,' said the man.

'But you're English.'

'Yes.'

'And the mayor?'

'Yes.'

Serge was dumbfounded.

'I think it might be best if you both stop telling stories and leave, don't you?' said the woman darkly.

I started the van and Serge climbed in zombie-like beside me. I pulled away, sticking my head out of the window.

'Bye then,' I said, accelerating up the drive.

But they had turned away and were disappearing into the house.

We drove along in silence. Serge appeared deeply troubled. After a while, he said, 'They were a bit snobby, weren't they?'

He was right. What an understatement. It was indicative that the French had to borrow an English word to describe a characteristically English attitude. They were bloody snobs all right.

We were entering a village. 'Pull over here,' said Serge pointing to a cafe, 'I need a drink.'

We sat at the bar while he revived himself with a stiff brandy.

There was a young English couple talking in loud voices at a nearby table and a party of friends joined them and started ordering drinks and laughing loudly together.

'You get a lot of English in here?' I asked the cafe owner in French.

'You're not joking,' he said. 'The place is full of English. In fact, even the mayor's English.'

'We know, we just met him,' said Serge hollowly.

'Well, he's not what you might call really English, more of an Anglophile. He's actually French but he grew up in England and married an Englishwoman,' said the owner. 'He gets on well with all the English in the commune and they voted him in. He's all right, but his wife's a right dragon.'

'We know, we met her too,' I said.

'Don't get me wrong, I'm not knocking it; English money's as good as anybody's. But house prices have shot up. Our young people can't afford to buy here any more. My son and his wife have had to build their own place two villages away. It's beginning to cause bad feeling.'

I'd heard about this. When the English first began buying up all the old properties the French were delighted to unload them for what they thought were extortionate prices, as the young French, bored with country life and lack of jobs, moved to the larger towns. At least the English were white Europeans (if they'd been Arabs it would have been a different story) and were generally polite and enamoured with *la vie française*. But now the sheer number of Brits was starting to change the landscape forever. Resentments were building. There had even been critical exposés of the phenomenon on the telly.

As we walked back to the van I noticed there were a lot of pasty overweight people in shorts and straw hats strolling about. Normally a French village like this would be dead so soon after lunch.

We were driving through the outskirts when a police wagon overtook and signalled us to pull over.

'Mother of Jesus,' said Serge. 'What have we done now?'

I stopped and a pair of formidable-looking gendarmes climbed out. 'Leave me to do all the talking, Johnny,' said Serge under his breath. 'I know what to say to *les flics*.'

My confidence in Serge's ability to deal with the police was nil from previous experience, and looking at these two I was even more sure he had no chance. They didn't even bother with: 'Would you mind kindly stepping out of the vehicle, sir?' One of them pulled the van door open and almost yanked Serge from his seat. The other hustled me out and we were pushed unceremoniously up against the side of the van. I was very conscious of the heavy pistols holstered in their shiny leather belts.

'*Pièces d'identité,*' demanded one of them, holding out his hand.

Serge, who looked cowed, needless to say couldn't find his.

The gendarme took this very badly. He looked as if he might become violent, given the slightest excuse.

He turned on me. 'What about you then?'

I felt for my *carte de séjour*, shitting myself that I might have forgotten it. I located it in my back pocket and handed over the laminated card.

He examined it closely and checked me against the photo. 'Where do you live?'

I reeled off the address.

'It says here you're a foreigner. Where are you from?'

'England,' I said.

'Yes, OK, but whereabouts?'

'London originally.'

'You like living here in France?'

'Yes, it's good. The people are very nice.' (Slime, slime – creep, creep, I thought, hating myself for being so pathetic.)

He pondered this. His attitude seemed to be softening slightly.

'Your French isn't that bad. I thought you were a Belgian.'

I wasn't sure whether to take this as a compliment or not.

He rounded on Serge. 'So you're leading this Englishman astray, are you? What have you been up to, you halfwit?'

Serge registered innocent surprise. 'Up to? We haven't been up to anything, officer.' He was hurt at being called a halfwit.

The other gendarme had been rummaging around in the front of the van and emerged holding the bronze figurine.

'Where did you nick this from then?'

'We just bought that,' said Serge. 'We paid for it fair and square.'

Our gendarme looked incredulous.

'It's the God's honest truth,' said Serge. 'Up the *déchetterie*. Ask that cowboy bloke who runs it. He sold it to us.'

'What, Lucky Luke?' Our gendarme took the bronze figurine from his partner. 'Very nice.' He was smiling despite himself. 'I can see why you'd want to nick it.'

'We didn't nick it,' insisted Serge. He was unwisely growing slightly self-righteous about it. 'Go and check with that bloke... that Lucky Luke character – whatever his name is – up the *déchetterie* if you don't believe me.'

They looked at him like he was dirt, hardly worth bothering with.

Our gendarme came over to me. 'Is this true? Did you get this from Lucky Luke up the *déchetterie*?'

I nodded. He pulled me to one side.

'Why are you hanging around with this little shit? It's not really a good idea.'

I explained how I was just starting out and Serge was showing me the ropes.

'Yeah, well, my advice is get someone else to help you. This idiot's a heap of trouble.'

He pulled open the doors of the police wagon. 'OK, in the back, you.' He was talking to Serge, who hesitated, looking shocked.

'Are you arresting us, officer?'

They ignored him.

'You too.' He was talking to me. We both got in and sat on the bench seat next to each other. We pulled away and they turned on the flashing blue light and siren. They probably didn't get many chances to use them.

I looked at Serge and he gave me a reassuring grin. Was that gendarme right? Maybe I shouldn't be hanging around with him. It was true he was a bit of a rogue but 'little shit' was laying it on a bit strong.

We arrived at the *déchetterie* in a cloud of dust, lights blazing, siren wailing. The dog on a string set up a frantic barking and Lucky Luke emerged from his hut, his eyes wide in disbelief.

We watched from the wagon as the gendarmes questioned him.

They showed him the bronze and gestured back at us. He shook his head, slowly at first. Then as they continued to quiz him he held his hands out, shrugging and shaking his head emphatically. He looked over at us curiously as if he'd never seen us before.

'He's denying it,' said Serge, 'the arse-licking ponce.'

Our gendarme strolled over grimly. 'He says he's never seen either of you or the bronze before.'

Serge stuck his head out of the window and shouted at the top of his voice: 'What about the hundred euros I paid you? Tell them what you've done with that, you wanker!'

'That'll do,' said our gendarme. 'We don't want this to degenerate into a slanging match.'

'The guy's a complete arsehole,' said Serge. 'It's obvious he's lying.'

'Possibly, but if he won't corroborate your story there's nothing we can do about it.'

'It's come to something,' said Serge, 'when a bloke can't go about his business without being arrested at the drop of a hat.'

'And you can shut up, you little shit!' The other gendarme had come back over. He looked ready for a bit of gratuitous violence. 'The mayor isn't keen on filth such as yourself touting round his commune conning innocent citizens out of their valuables.'

Our gendarme, who was more sympathetic, turned to me. 'Look, was it really such a good idea to go round and bother the mayor like that? His wife phones and we have to do something about it. She's always on at us... We never get a moment's peace.'

'What, that old dragon?' said Serge. 'What does she know about France or us, the French people?'

I thought he'd already gone too far, but he was incensed, getting into his stride.

'So that's it now, is it? Foreigners calling the shots and we have to jump? Le Pen was right, France is being ruined.'

Our gendarme nodded in agreement. 'We're just doing our job. We're not paid to think.'

'What about my bronze?' said Serge.

'That's confiscated,' said the other gendarme. 'We'll check it out and if it's been reported stolen you'll be in deep water.'

Serge opened his mouth to protest, but thought better of it. I began to wonder where Lucky Luke had got it from. If he'd nicked it we were both in trouble. I was still worrying about it as they drove us back to our van and dropped us off.

As they were about to leave us, our gendarme beckoned me over.

'Don't forget, best distance yourself from your little *copain* there. He'll drag you down, believe you me.'

I looked across in embarrassment at Serge to see if he'd heard, but he was staring vacantly ahead.

'And if either of you come within farting distance of this commune again you're dead men,' said the other one.

We watched them drive off.

Serge was livid. As we trudged all the way back to our van he swore imaginatively about the gendarmes and Lucky Luke. Then he turned the full heat of his fury on what he described as the snobby English.

He cursed the mayor and he cursed his dragon of a wife.

Then he cursed all the thousands of English in France and bemoaned how they were ruining everything.

'But I don't count you in all this, Johnny,' he said, apologetically. 'You're not one of them, are you? You're more like one of us.'

He raised his fist in the air, yelled, 'France up the mountain!' and began singing an obscure patriotic song.

Was he right? Was I more like him? I was beginning to question exactly where my loyalties lay. I knew one thing for sure – they weren't with that high-and-mighty mayor and his snotty wife.

'And by the way, Johnny, how come your royal family are so *ugly*?' He pulled a face.

'I'm not talking about Princess Diana. She was beautiful. At least you've got two handsome princes now thanks to her. Harry and William are fine-looking young men. But look at the rest of them. Charles and Anne – they're like gargoyles.'

Amazing. He appeared to know more about the British royal family than I did. But he had a valid point, even if I couldn't agree with him completely.

We climbed back in our van and drove along in silence for a while, until he said, 'Well, we can kiss that bronze and my hundred euros goodbye.'

'Do you think it was stolen?'

'Probably. Or maybe someone dumped it without knowing what it was worth. Either way, we'll never see it again.'

He began to hum 'La Marseillaise' softly at first, and then louder, breaking into song.

Allons enfants de la Patrie
Le jour de gloire est arrivé!
Contre nous de la tyrannie!
L'étendard sanglant est levé

'La Marseillaise' is one of those great anthems, like 'The Red Flag', impossible to ignore. I tried to resist but I couldn't help myself. I found myself joining in, singing along enthusiastically until we were both yelling out the verses, waving our fists in the air.

We finished and I caught Serge looking at me with a benign grin on his face. 'See, Johnny, you sing 'La Marseillaise' like a Frenchman. In your heart, here,' he thumped his chest, 'you are French.'

I considered this for a moment. Could he be right? It was a hard thing to have to admit to myself – but maybe I was starting to turn native.

We drove along in silence for a while until Serge broke into 'La Marseillaise' again. He appeared to have forgotten all about the bronze figurine and his money. I glanced across at him singing away and smiling to himself and realised I was actually starting to grow quite fond of the 'little shit'.

7

HERCULES

We were still singing 'La Marseillaise' together, driving down a gently winding road through a shady glade of trees, when Serge suddenly stopped.

'Hang on, Johnny, slow down, there's a dog ahead.'

I'd already seen it, a short-legged, rough-coated hunting dog with long floppy ears and a bell on its collar. It was trotting along in the middle of the road, looking fearfully over its shoulder.

I slowed to a crawl, but instead of heading off for the verge out of our way it scurried along faster.

'Pull over,' said Serge. 'We're only frightening it.'

I stopped the van and cut the engine.

'Some peasant's taken it out hunting in the woods and it's got lost. If we can catch it it's probably got a collar tag.'

We climbed out and set off down the road on foot whistling and calling. The animal seemed to be spooked by our interest and hurried along with its tail between its legs, bell jingling.

The way ahead led down to a stone bridge with a metal handrail crossing a narrow river tributary. The dog approached this with trepidation, slowing down as if unsure of what to do.

'I hate to see a little mite lost and scared like this,' said Serge. He dropped down on one knee and began cooing out terms of endearment.

This appeared to have the desired effect. The dog hesitated. Its ears pricked up. Maybe it had misjudged us.

'Come on, it's all right, *copain*. We won't hurt you.' Serge was using his most cajoling voice.

The dog sat down in the middle of the road. It watched with interest as he crept forward on his knees, making encouraging kissy noises.

Then we heard it – the unmistakable sound of a car approaching. In the calm of the surrounding woodland we could hear the gear change and the whine of the motor as it began to climb. A heavy, white, highly polished saloon appeared over the brow of the hill and came sweeping down the road. Dappled reflections from the overhanging trees scrolled across the windscreen. A deep purr from the engine as it gathered speed.

The dog got up and trotted onto the bridge. We waved and shouted, but instead of braking the car accelerated.

The front bumper caught the dog with a thunk, lifting it bodily, sending it twisting in mid-air. It came down on the front of the bonnet, slid off and rolled under the wheels.

I couldn't believe what I had just witnessed. The driver must have seen the dog but had deliberately ignored it, as if it was of no worth. It was a heartless thing to do. I felt a rush of pity. And then I wanted to get at whoever had done it and make them pay.

Serge had the same reaction. We ran down the road screaming obscenities.

As the car drew nearer we could see the driver, a middle-aged woman with blonde hair, red lipstick and gold earrings. There was a man next to her in the passenger seat.

We charged, forcing it to slow down. The window was lowered and the man leaned across the woman. He looked scared.

I shouted in English, I was so angry: 'You idiot. You fucking idiot! You killed it!'

The woman appeared nervous but unmoved.

'*C'était pas ma faute.*' (It wasn't my fault.)

She wasn't the least bit sorry. She was almost smug. Her reaction was unforgivable. I saw red and tried to grab her. Serge had hold of the handle, pulling the door open.

I gripped the woman's arm but the man grappled with me and began shouting at the woman to drive off. The window came up, forcing me to let go as the car leaped forward, almost running me over.

The pair of us were left staggering, cursing impotently as it disappeared round the bend. We stood listening for a moment, trying to get our breath. Then all was peaceful again, as if nothing had happened.

'What filth!' shouted Serge. 'May she rot in hell for all eternity.'

Still shaken, we started back down towards the bridge. The dog was lying on its side with a small pool of blood on the road by its half-open jaws. It must have died almost instantly without knowing what had hit it. We carried the still warm body to the verge and Serge examined the collar tag.

'His name was Hercules and there's a phone number,' he said. He tapped it out on his mobile and waited.

'I didn't tell you, Johnny, but he's just like my old Danton. The same sort of dog, almost the same colour. How could anyone do such a thing?' There were tears of frustration welling up in his eyes.

Someone answered the phone and Serge began to explain what had happened. He pulled out a Bic and wrote an address down on the palm of his hand.

'It's only in the next village. Poor old Hercules was on his way home.'

We picked up the body, placed it gently in the back of the van and set off.

The house was on the outskirts of the village, set back up a dirt road. There was a woman in a blue floral pinafore waiting by the wrought-iron front gate and when she saw us she gave a little wave of acknowledgement. She called out to someone in the house and a man appeared in his shirtsleeves and braces. We opened the back of the van and showed them the body.

'Dear old Hercules, I was worried something had happened to him,' said the woman. 'He often got lost but he always made it back on his own before.' Her voice cracked. 'He was a good boy.'

When Serge tried to explain what had happened he broke down and began to sob uncontrollably. The woman put her arm round his shoulder and we helped him into the house. The man poured a brandy and Serge swigged at it.

'If only we could have done something.' He was distraught, tears streaming down his face. 'I'm so sorry. Please forgive us. There was nothing we could do.'

I explained how he had recently lost his own dog, a similar breed to Hercules, and they listened as I told them about the accident. There was a strength between them, as if they were used to facing small tragedies like this together.

When I'd finished the man excused himself and went to fetch a plastic tarpaulin to wrap the body in.

By the time he returned Serge had almost managed to pull himself together. He knocked back the glass of brandy and accepted a top-up. He still looked upset though. His eyes were red and he had to keep blowing his nose.

I could hear the man and woman talking together in the kitchen. They came back in and the woman said she wanted to show us something out in the barn. Serge got up with his brandy in hand and we followed her out to the courtyard and through a weather-beaten door into a stone building which smelled of straw and cows. She led us over to a cattle stall with waist-high worn wooden partitioning. There was a rustling and snuffling followed by the scratching of tiny claws against the panel. She reached over and pulled out a puppy by the scruff of its neck.

'This is one of the last of Hercules' pups.' She thrust the small animal at Serge. He passed me his drink and took it in his arms. He was taken aback, unsure how to react. Used to feeling he had the upper hand when dealing with people he classed as rustics or peasants, he'd shown a softer side of himself and I had the impression he felt at a disadvantage.

'He's eight weeks old and ready to leave his mum. He needs someone like you to give him a good home.'

'Oh, I don't know if I'm quite ready to...'

He threw me a resigned look and then grinned goofily as the puppy struggled and licked his face.

'Go on, Serge, he likes you,' I said. The puppy was biting his collar.

'We'd like you to have him,' said the woman. 'You've been so kind about our Hercules.'

Serge was holding the little animal gently. It had stopped wriggling and was nuzzled up against his neck. 'I suppose he is a bit of a sweetie.'

He'd melted. He was keeping the dog.

We went back into the kitchen and sat chatting as the woman plied us with coffees, slices of home-made chocolate tart and sugared almonds. Serge had perked right up. He was almost back to his old self with his new friend fast asleep on his lap.

'That's quite a nice old buffet you've got there,' he said. 'Have you ever thought of selling it?'

I glared at him but he ignored me. I couldn't believe he'd said it.

'I could offer you a good price for it. Cash of course. A bit of ready cash always comes in handy, doesn't it?'

Ten minutes later we were waving them goodbye with the buffet loaded in the back. I felt stunned. Serge held the puppy up and waved its little paw at them and blew kisses. He was gleeful about his new pal, happier than I'd ever seen him.

We drove off through the country lanes towards home. Eventually he said, 'It's been a strange day, hasn't it, Johnny?'

I agreed that it had.

'I'll never forgive that woman for killing that dog.'

'Me neither,' I said.

'Still, it's not all bad. I've got my new little friend here.'

I couldn't hold it in any longer.

'How could you do that?' I blurted out. 'How could you take advantage of those poor people when they were so down?'

He didn't know what I was talking about.

'The buffet!'

'What about it?'

'Did you have to con them?'

'Con them?' He was indignant. 'I never conned them. It was a business transaction. You saw them, they were happy enough to get the money.'

It was pointless pursuing it. He had no idea.

We drove along in silence until he said, 'I've thought of a name for him, Johnny. I'm going to call him Robespierre. What do you think?'

'Good,' I said. 'I like it.'

'Not too severe is it? You know the real Robespierre wasn't really a very nice character.'

'I was just thinking,' I said.

'What?'

'It would be a good name for you.'

'How do you mean?'

'Robespierre Bastarde... perfect!'

He hadn't a clue what I was on about, but he didn't like my tone.

'Let me remind you, Johnny, when I sell that buffet half the profit is yours. Share and share alike. It's hard to survive in this game. We're out working here. You have to grab at every chance you get.'

'I don't want it, you keep it,' I snarled.

We drove along in silence until I dropped him off. We parted on a very cold 'au revoir'.

Later, on my way home, the accident kept playing and replaying vividly in my head. I couldn't shake it off. The bumper catching Hercules; his body twisting in mid-air, sliding down the bonnet and rolling under the wheels. I felt a burning anger at the blonde woman with the lipstick and gold earrings. I wanted her to suffer for what she had done. I tried to remember exactly what she looked like so that if I ever saw her again I could confront her and make her pay.

I began to realise I had been traumatised by what I had witnessed. Serge had too, and I felt sorry for him – but that thing with the buffet.

An early memory popped up. It was of my first dog, the one I had befriended when I was a child on holiday. He was a beautiful long-haired red setter called Bruce and I had played with him every day on the beach. He grew so attached to me that his owners agreed to let us adopt him as they couldn't cope with him for some reason and, to my great joy, we were able to take him home with us at the end of the holiday.

I loved that dog with a passion and I would fall asleep cuddled up to him in his basket. Bruce was the first of many wonderful dogs that have given me so much love and pleasure over the years. When I thought of all the mongrels, Labrador retrievers and processions of Staffordshire bull terriers that have enriched my life I felt like crying.

And there it was again – the unwelcome graphic footage of Hercules, twisting in mid-air, sliding down the bonnet and rolling under the wheels of the big, shiny white saloon car.

I thought about Spike, our big old brindle Staffordshire bull terrier, an alpha male who had played such an important role in our lives for over twelve years both here in France and during the time we spent in Portugal. He had moved out from England with us and our two other Staffs – his mum Pugsley and his 'auntie' Lily – and throughout this time he had looked after us all and been a constant source of pleasure and support.

He had died not long since and Helen and I were still grief-stricken. He started to have epileptic fits soon after his mum died and would keel over and pass out, his limbs shaking involuntarily. He had to take epilepsy tablets and then cortisone as his legs became infected and swollen.

While Helen was in England visiting family and friends, he became so ill I had to make the difficult decision on my own at the vet's to have him 'put down'. The way he'd bravely gone into the surgery, greeting the vet and pleased to see him, broke my heart. The memory of burying his still-warm body under the apple tree in our orchard in the pouring rain suddenly got to me and I began to sob, wiping away the tears so that I could see to drive.

When I got home Helen was waiting. She was tired and had been out at an auction all day, but she immediately realised something was wrong.

It was a beautiful evening and we sat outside in the courtyard behind our house, watching the sun set as I told her all about my day. She was as upset as I was when I described what had happened to Hercules.

'How could someone do something like that?' she said. 'It seems so cold-blooded, inhuman. And a woman as well.'

'It's like the world's gone mad,' I said. 'It sort of destroys your faith in humankind. Not that I've got much faith in humankind anyway. We're just a load of jumped-up monkeys as far as I can tell.'

'You know, I think about Spike and then my mum and dad,' said Helen. 'It makes me feel so bad sometimes, I just look in the sky and hope for some sort of sign to let me know everything's all right, and they're sort of still there, looking over us. I know it sounds mad or desperate, but...'

We heard a thrumming sound. Three horses came galloping up the field that slopes down to the lane behind the house; a stallion, a mare and a foal. They stopped right in the middle, breathing hard, magnificent, backlit by the setting sun.

We looked on in silence and awe. Then they turned and walked slowly and quietly away as if they'd never been there. We looked at one another in disbelief.

'There are no horses free here, are there?' I said.

'No.'

'Then I think that was the sign that everything's all right.

'I think so too,' said Helen.' She squeezed my hand. 'I think those three have escaped from the pony club across the river. But, yes, I believe it was a sign.'

'So do I,' I said.

The ancient bell in the village church across the fields began to toll and the bats that nest under the tiles in our roof started to emerge one by one, flitting across the courtyard.

8

TEDDY BEARS

I didn't see Serge again until the Dax *brocante* market a fortnight later. He was lounging back in a battered Voltaire chair puffing away on a cigarette.

'How's Robespierre?' I enquired.

'Marvellous, Johnny. He's settled in like a dream, honestly. He went straight for my Danton's old dog bed like it belonged to him. I can't get him out of it. It's uncanny.'

I still felt a burning resentment about the buffet he'd bought from the old couple. I wanted to have a right go at him about it. But what was the use?

I absent-mindedly picked up an ancient brown teddy bear wedged in among all the dusty junk he had strewn out on the ground in front of him on a piece of blue plastic sheeting. It had the elongated pointed nose and long arms of a typical early teddy bear. The fur was worn away from generations of being cuddled.

'That's an antique teddy bear you've got there,' he said. 'They go like *petits pains*. I can't get enough of them.'

I looked inside its ear. I didn't know much about bears but this looked very much like a Steiff. I'd seen them before in auctions and they usually had the little Steiff button sewn inside the ear. It wasn't there now, but that didn't prove anything. I was aware that bears made by the German Steiff company were the most valuable and sought-after by collectors;

I held it up to my nose and gave it a surreptitious sniff. It smelled funky. As if it had been endlessly hugged and possibly dropped in a dog basket at some stage and slept on. The price on the ticket was quite steep.

'Where did you find him then?' I asked, thinking he probably conned some poor little kid to get it.

He got up and took the bear from my hands. 'He's nice, isn't he? You like him... you can have him, Johnny. I'll give you a special discount.'

But I wasn't interested. In fact, I was starting to think that I'd had more than my fill of Serge. I replaced the bear and headed back to my stand.

It was proving to be a quiet morning at the monthly Dax *brocante* market. Dax is a spa town attracting a large number of *curistes* who come for the mud baths and natural hot springs. They are known as *curistes* as they are here for the cure and to improve their health through the natural treatments on offer in the town. It is a bit of a shock when you first see them unselfconsciously striding around the town centre in slippers and towelling dressing gowns as if they've just fallen out of bed.

The efficacy of the natural springs is reputed to have been discovered by a Roman soldier who was off to war, and, unable to take his rheumatic old dog with him, went to drown him in the river. The dog emerged with his rheumatism gone and acting like a puppy again. It's too good a story to ignore, whether true or not, and they've erected a life-sized bronze statue of the legionnaire and his dog in the town. The cure is available on the health system and consequently the *curistes* are the lifeblood of Dax.

Recently the French health minister intimated that the health system would no longer pay for such treatments, but there was a massive outcry from the spa towns and he was obliged to eat his words.

We *brocanteurs* also benefited from the *curistes*. They were our best customers in the Dax market, and after their treatments, bored and with time to kill, they tended to frequent the *brocante* market, searching for some little rare treasure to take back home with them.

But this morning they were thin on the ground.

Louis, on the next stall, who sold old postcards, antique books and 78 rpm records, pulled a face at me and raised his eyes to heaven.

'*C'est mort, eh, John?*'

He did what he always does when he's bored: cranked up his antique HMV gramophone and blasted out red-hot jazz across the market. It was the Lionel Hampton Big Band from the forties. A few bars of that and I'd cheered up enough not to care about selling. Anyway, the *curistes* were bound to turn up in the afternoon. They always had before.

Louis was bopping away, clicking his fingers out of time and singing along (we drummers tend to notice little things like that, like how white audiences have difficulty clapping along on the off-beat). But he was a big jazz fan, and could quote all the sidemen on every record.

He had ordered us paellas from a nearby restaurant for lunch and we sat around his portable table, eating and drinking, joking and listening to jazz.

I forgot all about Serge's teddy bear until I was on the way back later with a tray of coffees from the cafe and noticed it had gone. I felt a twinge of regret. I was sure it had been a genuine Steiff from the twenties and probably worth a few bob in auction back in the UK. He must have sold it before lunch and I almost began to wish I'd negotiated a fair price for it myself.

True to form, the market picked up in the afternoon and the *curistes* were out in force. I was heartened when they were predictably drawn to the colourful English tea sets we specialised in on our stall. The vision many French have of England and all things English is a strange one. England, they imagine, is the quaint chintzy world of Agatha Christie's Miss Marple mysteries; little villages inhabited by old-fashioned characters scurrying about their business, cut off from the twenty-first century. They are charmed especially by our floral-patterned English china, although the word 'china' often confuses them. French china is called *porcelaine* and when they initially see 'china' on the bottom of an English teacup or saucer they believe it to have been made in China. This is not what they are after, however 'charming' it is. A detailed explanation of how the first porcelain brought to England came originally from China, and how the English have used the word 'china' to describe porcelain ever since, often convinces them, but not always. We were once at an antiques fair near Bordeaux where an 'expert' was paid by the fair's organisers to go round from stall to stall to verify that all items on sale were genuine antiques and not modern copies. He took strongly against our tea sets which he insisted were made in China and not to be displayed. No amount of protestations or historical explanations would convince him otherwise. Louis said the man was an expert of *picolé*, pointing at his mouth with his thumb and imitating a drunkard draining a bottle of wine. Much incensed we left the china where it was and the 'expert' must have decided he was out of his depth because he never returned to insist we remove it. But the next time we returned to the fair we photocopied the translation of china and porcelain from the English–French dictionary and displayed it with dayglo highlights for him to see.

Here at Dax, a lady *curiste* bought a 'Country Roses' tea set from me, enthusing how charmingly English it was and how she loved to serve her friends tea from English china. As I packed it up for her Serge rode past on a prehistoric three-wheeled bike, wearing a Nazi helmet and singing an old French music hall song at the top of his voice. He had a coach horn with a rubber bulb in one hand and he was parping it loudly at anyone who got in his way.

'He's been at the bottle since lunch,' said Louis. 'It's not good when he carries on like this, he frightens the customers.'

He reappeared later, propelling himself along face down on a rusty old metal cart for the handicapped, the type of vehicle I would have imagined a destitute leper in Mumbai might use to get about on. His chin was a few inches off the ground and he was yelling at the top of his voice.

As he rolled past I leaned down and tapped him on the shoulder. 'You sold your teddy bear then, Serge?'

He stopped the cart and jumped up. 'So you noticed, eh, Johnny?' He leaned against me slurring his words. 'You missed out there, *copain*. I let him go cheap to a charming young mum, a birthday present for her little boy.'

The disappointment must have shown on my face because he glanced around and whispered conspiratorially. 'Never mind, Johnny. We'll meet up for a drink and a spot of lunch next week. I'll show you some more secrets of the trade.'

He dropped back down onto his cart and worked the pedals with his hands, driving himself forward. As he shot past the legs of a fat man examining postcards on Louis's stall, he twisted round and bawled back at me: 'Don't forget, Johnny, give me a call and we'll arrange it!'

Louis came over to check if his prospective customer had been alarmed. But the man was amused. I had noticed the French reaction was more often than not to welcome any unusual diversion and enjoy its entertainment value.

I thought no more of Serge's invite. I assumed he was drunk and would forget all about it. But after the weekend he called me on my mobile.

'Eh, Johnny, I thought you were going to phone me and come out for lunch?'

Maybe I'd been a bit harsh on him. He sounded genuinely hurt.

'I wanted you to come and meet some friends,' he said. 'What about tomorrow, how would that suit you?'

He sounded so disappointed I agreed to a rendezvous in a small Basque village in the foothills of the Pyrenees.

'I'll meet you outside the church at eleven-thirty, Johnny. Fantastic!'

I arrived in the picturesque village with its whitewashed buildings and Basque red-painted woodwork just after eleven o'clock. Serge was already there waiting for me by the church in his van.

'Eh, Johnny, let's have a quick aperitif before lunch.'

He guided me into the local Auberge, ordered himself a Ricard and a coffee for me and we sat outside enjoying the midday sun. He took a big sip of his Ricard, glanced around as if to check if anyone was listening and leaned across the table.

'There's a couple of things you need to know before you meet my girlfriend, Johnny.'

Oh, so it was his girlfriend, was it? I was wondering what we were up to.

'There are certain facts I want you to be clear on,' he said. 'So you don't blurt out anything that maybe it would be best she didn't know about me. Do you understand what I'm trying to say?'

I didn't, but I was getting an inkling.

'Believe it or not I've only been seeing this woman for a few weeks. I answered her ad in the lonely hearts column of the local paper. Her husband died a while ago and she's been very lonely. Living cut off in the country miles from anywhere, you don't tend to meet anyone nice.' He chuckled as if he couldn't believe his own luck.

'She's never been to my apartment, you know, where I do up my furniture and run my business. I try and keep that side of my life separate. You know, worlds collide. We don't want that, do we?'

I wasn't sure what he was on about but reluctantly assured him I wasn't going to blab out any of his sordid little secrets.

'Good, good. I knew I could trust you, Johnny.'

He slapped me on the back, finished his Ricard and stood up. 'Come on then, let's go have lunch.'

As I drove along trying to keep up with his van on the country lanes, I told myself I wasn't going to get involved in any more of his tawdry personal intrigues.

We turned off onto a bumpy dirt track and arrived at the house in a cloud of dust to be greeted by a pack of dogs. When I pulled up I heard the rattle of claws as they jumped up against the side of my van. And as I climbed out I was surrounded and given a wild welcome by a noisy chorus ranging from high yelps to deeply gruff barks. There were dogs of all shapes and sizes. Most of them were of the floppy-eared short-legged hunting variety of the region. But I recognised Scotties, Labradors and a pair of big brown Beaucerons, the wonderful shepherd dogs so much favoured by French country people.

They accompanied us, still barking, as Serge led me up to a big old stone house much like the one I lived in myself. The roof was covered in moss and weeds, the *crépi*, or stone-coloured rendering on the walls, had seen better days, and some of the shutters were hanging off their hinges. But there were freshly painted pots of brightly flowering geraniums lined up along the stone pathways.

A group of children were playing with a goat on a patch of grass. Two of the younger ones stopped when they saw us and came running over. There was a rough-sawn wooden table round the back laid out with plates, chequered napkins and cutlery. Serge waved for me to be seated and one of the toddlers tried to climb on my knee while he disappeared into the house. The rest of the children, seemingly tired of playing with their goat, came over to have a good look at me. I got the impression from their faces that they weren't used to seeing many strangers.

Serge came back out with an attractive woman whom he introduced as Regine. She was dark and vivacious and much younger than he was. She blushed as she shook my hand and when she had gone back in to fetch our lunch Serge said, 'She's beautiful, isn't she, Johnny?'

'Yes,' I said.

'Don't forget what I told you.' He made the sign of the zipped up mouth.

I looked across at all the children, who, deciding I wasn't that interesting anyway, had gone back to playing with the goat.

'It's great having a ready-made family like this, isn't it?' said Serge, following my gaze. It's a school holiday today so they're running wild with some of their little pals.

He shouted out for them to come in and get washed for lunch and Regine came back out with baskets of hot bread, garlic butter and plates of duck pâté and crudités.

'Hang on,' said Serge, 'we need a good bottle of wine to cheer us up. Come and help me choose one, Johnny.'

It didn't seem like the moment to remind Serge I was a reformed alcoholic sworn off the booze, so I trailed after him through a sitting room with its distinctive Basque carved wooden furniture, crimson-painted walls and large *cheminée* (a fireplace with a chimney).

I noticed an antique teddy bear perched up on the mantelpiece not dissimilar to the one I had seen on his stall.

I went to ask him about it but he had disappeared. His voice floated up from below.

'Come on, Johnny, down here!'

I descended a stone stairway into a cool cellar stretching under the house. By the light of the suspended naked light bulbs I could see the walls were lined with dusty bottles of wine in wooden racks. And at the far end there was a row of large wooden barrels upended with taps in the side.

'Regine's husband Jean-Pierre did all this,' he said. 'You know sometimes I find myself offering him up a little prayer of thanks for all the good things he left behind for me. I know I don't deserve it, but I feel he should know how much I appreciate it.'

He pulled out a couple of bottles and blew off the dust, revealing yellowed hand-written labels. 'Ah, yes, these will do. Thank you, Jean-Pierre.'

He examined the label closely. 'He had good taste, Jean-Pierre did. I think we're going to enjoy this.'

We re-emerged, blinking in the bright sunshine with Serge clutching the bottles. I completely forgot to ask him about the teddy bear on the mantelpiece.

He pulled the corks and poured the wine and we sat looking out over green fields full of wild flowers stretching as far as the eye could see. The giant shadow of the Pyrenees loomed in the distance. I couldn't imagine a better setting for lunch nor a more idyllic spot to live and bring up a family.

Regine brought out an enamel pot of rabbit stew and a plateful of plain, unadorned white rice for me with a side salad of sliced tomatoes. I watched Serge tucking enthusiastically into the rabbit while I picked away at the flavourless grains.

'This is wild rabbit,' he said. 'Much nicer than the tame ones.' He waved towards some concrete hutches where I could see several little brown rabbits hopping about. 'I picked up this little fellow on the road last night. He was still warm... clipped by a car.'

'You know, Johnny, life is not bad out here in the country, but sometimes it gets a little boring. If I couldn't work and tour around I'd probably end up doing myself in like the neighbour Marc over there.'

He pointed to a house tucked away beyond the sloping fields at least two or three kilometres away.

'His wife went off with the postman and he killed himself with his own chainsaw. Cut himself to pieces behind the barn. It was one hell of a mess, Regine tells me. They had to hose down the cobblestones.'

I tried not to imagine what killing yourself with your own chainsaw would be like. A lot of the peasants I met had fingers missing from various accidents but I'd not heard of anything like this before.

'Oh yes, the things that go on in these little villages would turn your hair white. It's not all a bed of roses, like some of you English imagine. Life can be hard and lonely, especially in the winter when the snow comes down. That's no picnic, I can tell you.'

Regine brought out a large *tarte aux pommes* and then went back inside, busying herself in the kitchen. How like Serge, I thought, to find himself a girlfriend who would wait on him hand and foot. We ate slices and drank cups of coffee. Serge tried to tempt me to try a glass of *eau-de-vie*, a potent home-made apple brandy. I took a small sip at his insistence and it nearly blew my head off. There was a time when I'd have downed it in one swift gulp and asked for more. I knew I had to be careful, but convinced myself I could handle a few sips, surely, without embarking on an out-of-control drinking binge.

Serge lit a cigarette and inhaled deeply. 'It's days like these I thank God for everything. I don't have to work too hard and the life of a *brocanteur* is an enjoyable one as long as you know all the wrinkles.'

He stood up, stretched and yawned.

'But I was going to let you in on some of my little secrets, wasn't I? See, I haven't forgotten.'

He gathered up a pile of dishes and we carried them through and plonked them in the sink in the kitchen. I could hear the whirr of an electric sewing machine in the next room and peeked through to see Regine and a teenage girl bent over, working. Regine looked up and smiled. She was sewing up brown furry material which I recognised as a potential teddy bear from the pattern, with a pointed snout and round ears.

'Eh!' said Serge, throwing up his hands in mock alarm. 'You've discovered my little secret, Johnny.'

There were two half-stuffed bears lying on the table. They were similar to the antique teddy bear, but brand new and in pristine condition. The teenage girl was doing something to a finished bear she was holding in her hand.

'That teddy on your stall was an antique,' I said. 'I'll never believe you made him here.'

'Believe what you like, Johnny, but I'm showing you my secrets and I'm trusting you not to reveal them to anyone.'

I watched the girl at work. She opened a cut-throat razor and began to shave particular parts on the head, body, arms and legs until she seemed satisfied with the result. Then she pushed the bear away and reached for another.

'This is just the early stages of my little production line,' said Serge.

He led me out back to a yard where two of the children I had seen earlier, a boy and a girl in blue dungarees, were scraping stuffed teddy bears against the stone walls of the house.

'This is what they call rubbing teddy,' he said. 'We've got to wear away a lot of that nice clean fur if we want them to look old.' He took the bear from the little girl's hand and examined it.

'Very good, Yvette. Just scuff it up a bit more and it'll be perfect.' He patted her head and handed it back.

'After that we roll them about in the dust for a bit and then they go in here for the final stages of my top secret process.'

He took me through to an outhouse where several of the dogs I had seen earlier were lying about. There were empty baskets and most had teddies instead of blankets in them.

A big old Bauceron bitch with limpid brown eyes half stood up when she saw Serge. She went to climb out of her basket and there were puppies hanging off her teats. Serge knelt down and fussed her, settling her back down. He took a puppy in one hand and stroked it.

'This is the final touch, the *pièce de résistance*.' He replaced the puppy, pulled out a teddy from the basket and sniffed it.

'Smell that.' He passed it to me.

'You can't fake that. That's the aroma of life.'

He was right. The teddy bear gave off a delicious doggy tang. And it looked as old and battered as the one I had admired on Serge's stall.

'This is amazing, Serge,' I said. 'I would have sworn this bear is genuine.'

'Ah yes, but that's because I had an original to copy.'

He went over to a pair of heavy oak doors in the lath and plaster wall, opened the cupboard and took out a teddy bear and passed it to me. It was the same as the others, save for one difference – its fur was black, not brown. It had a little Steiff button in its ear. It was worn in all the right places, decidedly and, as far as I could tell, an original antique Steiff bear. But now I had seen all Serge's reproductions I wasn't sure.

'This one is genuine?' I asked.

'It belonged to Regine's grandmother, who passed it on to her mother. Her mother grew up in Quebec. She met and married Regine's father on a visit to France. That's the real thing all right.'

If he was telling the truth, which I very much doubted, then this bear was an incredibly rare one. After seeing Serge's teddy bear the other day I'd looked out a book that Helen had at home which traced the history of the first teddy bears and the firms that manufactured them. There were several chapters about the celebrated German Steiff bears. Funnily enough, I'd been interested in the fact that black Steiff bears were extremely rare and that only about five hundred were manufactured in memory of the sinking of the *Titanic*. It seemed like a coincidence but I distinctly remembered reading that one of these black bears was sold at Christie's in London for nearly a hundred thousand pounds and now here I was apparently holding one. As I looked down at it in my hands it appeared to shimmer with an inner light. Its little beady eyes twinkled back at me.

I had to admit it looked genuine enough. But there again, was Serge testing me? Seeing how much of a mug I really was?

'Regine ever think of selling him?' I asked, nonchalantly.

'Why, you interested in buying him?'

'I don't know, there's always a possibility.'

He brought his face up close to mine. 'Maybe if you offered her a good price she might consider it.'

'Why, how much were you thinking of?'

'Oh, I don't know... maybe she could let him go for a million francs.' (Roughly one hundred thousand pounds sterling.)

Something in my expression must have struck him as funny because he erupted with laughter, bending over, almost choking on his cigarette smoke.

He recovered, stood up, pulled out a voluminous linen handkerchief and blew his nose.

'Money! What good is money? I never seem to be able to hang on to it anyway. The taxman comes chasing after it and people steal it before you get a chance to spend it. We'll just keep Regine's little teddy here in case the family need the cash for a rainy day.'

He replaced the bear carefully in the cupboard and locked the door. 'I trust you, Johnny. I don't know why. Just forget you ever saw him, OK?'

We went back outside and the sun was shining, the birds were singing. But I have to admit Regine's supposedly priceless black Steiff teddy bear was uppermost in my mind. I was pretty sure Serge was having a joke at my expense. The black bear was a fake and he'd set up the whole thing to see how much I really knew about antiques.

When it was time for me to go he insisted I take an armful of his home-made bears.

'No need to pay anything now,' he said. 'Just give me half of what you sell them for.'

The eau de vie had hit the spot. My senses were swimming and I tripped a couple of times on the way back to the car.

'Listen, Johnny,' said Serge. 'What about we make that expedition into the country this week? The one we keep promising ourselves. The weather forecast is good and we'll have a laugh. What do you say?'

'OK, Serge,' I said. 'Why not?'

'I'll give you a ring tomorrow and we'll sort it out,' he said.

Regine and the kids came out to see me off and as I bumped along the dirt track I could see them all in my rear-view mirror smiling and waving. The fake bears were bouncing around on the seat next to me and I was wondering just how many other little surprises Serge had hidden up his sleeve for me.

I arrived home in time to find Helen unloading boxes of 'smalls' (bric-a-brac, sadly, not frilly underwear) from our beaten-up Renault. I remembered she had been to an auction in Biarritz.

'What do you think of this?' she said, pulling out a crystal chandelier. 'Guess how much?'

'I don't know, about a tenner.'

'What planet are you living on?' she said, replacing it carefully in the box.

I was cradling a pair of Serge's faked-up teddy bears, cuddling them close.

'All right then, what do you think of these?' I asked. 'Sweet or what?'

'What are they for?'

'I thought we could sell them. Serge gave them to me. I just have to give him half the profit.'

'But they're fakes,' she said.

'Is it that obvious? I thought they were really good, just like the real thing.'

'Have you been drinking or what?' she said. 'I thought we agreed we weren't going to sell fakes.'

'So you wouldn't reckon they were genuine Steiff antique teddy bears then?'

'How much *have* you had to drink?' She was laughing but I sensed she was genuinely worried.

'I just had a little taste of eau de vie,' I explained.

'And the rest! We can't sell these. You'd better give them back to him. I think you've fallen for the classic antique mistake. You think you've found something worth a lot of money, you get swept up in the heat of the moment, you get excited and later in the cold light of day you get a reality check. Best not done in public but we all do it.'

I was disappointed, unwilling to concede I'd been duped. 'OK, but I think we should give Serge's bears a go. Where's the harm in it?'

'That's up to you, but the man's a complete idiot and I don't know why you're hanging about with him.'

Now she came to mention it, what was I doing hanging about with him? It's what everyone was saying. They were probably all right. I made a mental note to try and avoid him in future. When he phoned up in the week to arrange our little *'expédition'*, I was definitely going to put him off.

9

BULLFIGHTS AND MONKEY BUSINESS

It was a balmy morning in mid-October and it had taken me ages to find the bar in the old quarter of Bayonne. It was hidden away down a shady alley and at first I thought it was closed. But when I pushed the door it swung open and I found myself in what I can only describe as a chapel dedicated to the glory of the slaughter of bulls. The bar was called 'La Corrida' so I shouldn't really have been surprised to find it was crammed with all the paraphernalia of the bullring.

Against all advice I had agreed yet again to meet up with Serge and help him out. I was kicking myself for being a complete sucker, and thinking trust Serge to pick a place like this for a rendezvous.

I'd always believed Spain was the country where all the bullfighting went on. I'd even been to a bullfight as a 'bit of a lark' when a teenager on holiday there. Now there is a groundswell of opinion in Spain against the barbaric sport, with moves to ban it.

When I moved to France I was under the misapprehension that if there were any bullrings here then they didn't actually kill the bull. Just teased it a bit and then, after everyone had had their fun, released it back into the fields to recover and fight another day.

This is pure propaganda. Bullfighting is alive and well in southern France and growing in popularity, especially among the young. And the bulls are killed all right. When the season opens there are long queues outside the box offices and the local supermarkets always have a good supply of *daube de taureau* (slaughtered bull meat) for sale. Many little villages and towns have their own bullrings.

I ordered a coffee, seated myself at a corner table and tried not to look at the gory framed photos, posters and bulls' horns and ears that bedecked every spare inch of the walls.

Serge had phoned last week to tell me an old pal of his had tipped him off about a 'fantastic house clearance' that was going to 'earn us a fortune'. I was dubious, but figured maybe I'd give him another chance. What harm could it do? Now I was starting to wish I hadn't given in. When he still hadn't turned up three quarters of an hour later I decided to leave. Forget the whole thing.

Then he walked through the door with a character so downright thuggish and malodorous I immediately wished I'd followed my instincts and gone ten minutes earlier.

'Eh, Johnny.' Serge pumped my hand. 'Let me introduce to you my good friend, Bruno the Basque.'

The bloke reached out and when he gripped my hand I felt my flesh creep. The general impression he gave of seedy untrustworthiness wasn't helped by an ugly scar that ran right round his neck from ear to ear. My first thought was that someone had tried to cut his head off and failed. Then I guiltily realised the poor chap had probably undergone a terrible operation, possibly for throat cancer. But when he spoke his voice was strong with that throaty edge I'd noticed as being typical of some men of the Basque region and I returned to my original idea – someone had most likely tried to cut his head off.

'So, you're the *rosbif* Serge has told me so much about?' He held onto my hand and looked me up and down as if he were sizing me up.

'His name's Johnny,' said Serge with some irritation, 'not Rosbif. It's rude to call him Rosbif when you know his name's Johnny.'

I appreciated Serge defending me, but thought it a bit rich as he'd called me Rosbif many times himself, and I was aware he called me Johnny not John because he was a Johnny Hallyday fan.

I retrieved my hand and noticed I was involuntarily wiping it down the leg of my jeans. 'That's OK,' I said. 'It doesn't bother me, I'm used to it.'

'Yeah, they call us Froggy, so where's the harm in it?' said Bruno gruffly.

Serge called the barman over and ordered two Ricards and another coffee for me. 'It's not nice this term *rosbif*,' said Serge. 'So we eat frogs and you eat roast beef. Ha, ha, very funny. But this expression *rosbif* says more than you think. To a Frenchman it also mocks your complexion. It means rose beef, or red meat, which is a way of poking fun at what we see as your cherry-red skin. It's not nice at all and I don't like it.'

Bruno reached under the table and put his hand on my leg.

'OK, Serge, don't worry. I'll never call Johnny Rosbif again, not if you don't like it.' He leered at me and gazed deep into my eyes. He made me feel like I was a piece of meat, and I got a glimpse of how a woman must feel under the unwelcome gaze of a lecherous old man.

'Eh, I had that little mini-skirted whore who hangs round the Old Quarter last night,' he said turning to Serge. '*Truite crue!* As much as I wanted, as long as I wanted. Fantastic! And cheap too.' He grinned at me like I'd understand.

Serge laughed. 'You're a *gros mangeur*, Bruno. Aiyee! The last of the *gros mangeurs*. Come on, let's drink up and go. We've got work to do.'

They knocked back their Ricards and I was relieved to get out into the clean air. Serge and I followed Bruno's white Mercedes in my van as he drove out of Bayonne and into the open country.

'Robespierre OK?' I asked.

'He's fine. Settling in nicely. My next door neighbour is looking after him while I'm out. She's got nothing else to do and she loves animals.'

He lit up one of his Gitanes 'mais' cigarettes, with their distinctive yellow paper, much loved by French farmers and sons of the soil.

'Eh, Johnny, I think Bruno likes you.' He blew out a stream of acrid-smelling smoke. 'Don't take any notice of him, it's just his manner. I've known him since we played as lads together. He made a few mistakes later in life and got on the wrong side of the law. But he's still stayed my friend after all these years. He's not a bad person.'

You didn't have to be very bright to realise Bruno the Basque was the kind of old friend you'd be only too pleased to get rid of, and the sooner the better.

'What's *truite crue*?' I asked. I had a pretty good idea but wanted to hear it from Serge.

'It literally means "raw trout" – it's not a very nice expression,' he said prudishly. 'Bruno has some fairly earthy tastes when it comes to sex. He's not the sort of bloke you want to hang around in bars with late at night.'

'Don't worry, I won't,' I said.

'But if you ever want a gun of any sort – pistol, machine gun… whatever – he's the guy to get it for you. He's cheap too, and no questions asked. He brings them in from Eastern Europe and only deals in quality merchandise.'

I couldn't imagine a situation where I'd need to buy a gun off Serge's old buddy Bruno the Basque. But there again, you never know. Even so, I was getting a distinct feeling that agreeing to come on today's outing had been a big mistake.

The Merc had pulled off the road onto a dirt track, and we followed it through an oak wood until we came to a high stone wall where we pulled up in a cloud of dust.

Bruno and Serge got out and I watched them pointing and arguing together. If I backed up quickly and turned round I could drive off and leave them to it. I seriously considered the idea. But what about when I bumped into Serge at some market or other, which I was bound to do? I didn't think I could endure the embarrassment of explaining why I had run off.

They appeared to have come to a decision because Serge came back and climbed in beside me.

'OK, Johnny, Bruno got lost for a minute there. No problem, we just have to backtrack a bit and follow the road that runs parallel with the wall. We should come to a gate.'

We reversed out and did as he suggested. The mud track snaked through the woods, twisting and turning, with Serge shouting out in affirmation as he watched for signs of the wall through the trees. We came to a crossroads, turned off and arrived at an iron gate which was chained up with a hefty-looking padlock. They both got out and tried wrenching at it, without success. Eventually they gave this up and Bruno fetched an ugly-looking crowbar from the boot of his car and set about attacking it with frightening ferocity. But it was made of heavy iron and wasn't going to budge. Then they tried to lever the gate off its hinges but Serge caught his hand between the wall and the crowbar and leaped back and began hopping about swearing.

This wasn't good. If they legitimately had business here, why hadn't the owner given them a key? They appeared to be trying to break into private property. And where did that leave me? If the gendarmes arrived it would be useless to plead I didn't know what was going on. I'd be an accessory and the thought of being banged up in a cell with Serge's pal Bruno the Basque was the stuff nightmares were made of. I was about to tell them that maybe we should contact the owners and ask for a key when Bruno managed to break off one of the gate's hinges. Serge stopped sucking his hand and steamed in to finish the job. The pair of them huffed and puffed until they snapped the other hinge and swung the gate back in triumph.

Serge was jubilant as he climbed back in beside me and banged his good hand enthusiastically on the dashboard as we drove through the gate and followed Bruno's car across rolling parklands, through a small wood to emerge on a track crossing a rambling, overgrown garden. There were pitted pathways sprouting weeds and broken stone urns and unkempt rose bowers. And standing overlooking it all, alone and dishevelled like some hopeless, bedraggled aristocrat awaiting the guillotine, was a run-down eighteenth-century chateau. We pulled up on the potholed drive and looked up at the flaking stucco, smashed windows and dilapidated shutters.

'This is the place, all right,' said Serge. 'Bruno's mate the estate agent has sold it to some English people. The owner wanted to sell the chateau with all its contents and the English are paying such an overblown price for the place that Bruno's mate was able to convince the owner they'd bought the contents as well. Bruno's mate told the English people the price they were paying was for the empty chateau without the contents. So the owner thinks he's selling it full and the English think they've bought it empty. So that leaves a load of furniture and stuff all alone with no home to go to. Isn't that a shame, eh? And that's where we come in. Bruno's estate agent pal has asked us to remove the contents and split the value with him fifty-fifty. So then everyone's happy. The English are happy, Bruno's mate's happy, and we're happy.' He grinned at me.

It sounded like a clear case of fraud to me. But one that might be hard to prove.

I climbed out reluctantly and followed the pair of them round the crumbling building. It seemed cold and aloof as if it considered us unwelcome intruders. The only sound was the distant cawing of rooks and the crunch of our feet on the gravel. I could see we had arrived by the tradesmen's entrance because the main drive ran off in the distance through an avenue of towering poplar trees.

Bruno hammered on a side door, a pointless exercise, I thought, as no one could possibly be living in such a place. The noise echoed eerily and as we stood waiting and listening I half expected Herman Munster to appear and invite us in.

Then we heard shuffling and the clank of bolts being drawn back, and the door was opened by a snaggle-toothed woman with lank, greasy hair and nicotine-stained fingers. She was wearing a black Johnny Hallyday T-shirt, green leatherette miniskirt and carpet slippers.

She must have been expecting us because she ushered us straight in and led us down a dank corridor into an open hallway and through to a vast living room. Light shone through tattered pieces of blue plastic hanging over the broken windows and cast a cold glow on the dustsheet-covered furniture.

'Would you like anything?' she asked, throwing us a crooked smile. 'Something to drink, perhaps?'

'Later,' said Bruno brusquely, yanking off a dustsheet to reveal a settee covered in torn red plastic. He tried another and exposed a battered armchair in a similar state of repair.

'Holy mother of Jesus! This junk is going to need some sorting out.'

As we removed the rest of the dustsheets it became clear that any antique furniture the chateau had once boasted had been either stolen or sold off long ago. What we had here was an assortment of cheap crap; old chairs and tables that had been brought in to serve the building's various occupants. In every room it was the same story; junk only fit for carting up to the tip. Serge got excited briefly when he discovered a sixties-style cane chair hanging from a chain in a bedroom. But Bruno was unimpressed and left us to it saying he was going to check out the attic.

'Never mind,' said Serge. 'I thought it was too good to be true. Who would ever offer Bruno the chance to clear a chateau full of valuable antiques? You know, sometimes, Johnny, it doesn't do to be over-optimistic in life. This is no more than I expected. Maybe we can salvage something out of all this stuff. That hanging cane chair has got to be worth a few euros for a start.'

We had started to pile up all the bits and pieces Serge judged to be of any value in the hallway ready to load into the van, when Bruno reappeared on the stairs with a carrier bag in his hand.

'Hey, what have you got there then?' asked Serge. 'Anything good?'

'It's just some junk,' said Bruno pushing past.

'Come on, don't be shy. Let's have a look.' Serge followed him trying to get a glimpse inside.

'Hey, it looks like a lamp!' yelled Serge. 'Let's see it.'

'It's nothing, just a *pompe*, that's all.'

When Serge made a grab at it Bruno swung round and went to push him off. '*Putain!* Look out, you stupid idiot. You'll break it!'

'If it's only a fake then why are you so worried if it gets broken?'

'I'm not,' said Bruno. 'Here, see for yourself.' He placed the bag on the floor and allowed Serge to look in it.

'This is no *pompe*!' yelled Serge in disbelief. He lifted out an orange and blue lamp, turning it in the light, examining the glass. 'Look, it's signed Gallé just here. It's worth a small fortune.'

'Yeah, well it was hidden under some junk.' Bruno took it purposely from Serge's hands and replaced it carefully in the bag. 'It's only a fake, but you know – finders keepers.' He picked it up and headed out for his car, followed closely by Serge.

'Any idiot could tell it's a genuine Gallé,' said Serge. 'You agreed to share and share alike.'

Bruno opened the boot, placed the bag inside, shut the lid and went impassively round to get in the front of his car. Serge grabbed his arm and tried to pull him back.

'Bruno, I'm your friend. You can't treat me like this.' He was pleading now. 'There's plenty of profit in the lamp for both of us. Let's split it down the middle.' I couldn't help noticing that Bruno's estate agent pal and myself had been instantly cut out of the deal.

Bruno went to open his car door but Serge gripped him tightly round the waist trying to pull him back. This developed into a scuffle. Bruno pushed Serge violently in the chest, sending him sprawling onto the driveway.

I helped Serge up and we stood silently as Bruno climbed in the Merc and slowly wound down the window, grim-faced.

'Like I told you, I found the lamp so it belongs to *me*. I'm warning you, Serge, if you ever try to attack me like that again, you won't get off so lightly.'

He turned to me. 'And as for you, Rosbif...' His voice was like ice. 'I'm giving you fair warning, too. Don't you get any funny ideas.' I got a vision of all those guns he had at his disposal. He doubtless had a lethal weapon to hand in his car to blow me away if he felt like it.

He started the Merc, gunned the motor and accelerated off at speed, leaving behind a couple of deep wheel marks in the drive.

Serge stood up, dusting himself down and picking bits of gravel out of his arm.

'*Putain*, the filthy *con*! I don't like to tell you this, Johnny, but that lamp was worth a hell of a lot.'

'If it was a genuine Gallé…' I said.

'Oh, it was genuine, all right. It was easily worth the price of a brand new car. I can't believe Bruno would do something like this to me.'

I thought he was getting worked up over nothing and there was no way that was a real Gallé. Even to my untrained eye it looked like a clumsy imitation. But nothing I could have said would have persuaded Serge otherwise. And I wasn't surprised by Bruno the Basque's behaviour either. I was glad to be rid of him. He was welcome to the bloody lamp as far as I was concerned.

We watched the Merc disappearing up the avenue of poplar trees.

'Are you moving into the chateau today?'

We turned to see a miniature man dressed in seventies checked trousers, a floral shirt and tie, purple tank top and built-up shoes. My first thought was that we had slipped into another dimension and this was a leprechaun.

'You're the English people, aren't you? I'd be glad to give you a hand.'

I looked at Serge. He seemed dazed, as if he was still trying to come to terms with Bruno's betrayal and wasn't yet ready for any sudden surprises.

The little man cocked his head on one side. He had tomato pips stuck to his tie and a childlike smile.

'No, we're not moving in,' I said. 'I am English, but no, we're not moving in.'

This seemed to puzzle him. He frowned, trying to work it out.

'You are English though?'

'Yes.'

'But you're not moving into the chateau?'

'No.'

He frowned some more and then gave up.

'I live over there,' he said. He waved towards the avenue of poplar trees. 'Do you want to come and see my house?'

Did I want to come and see his house? No, not really.

'I've got cake,' he said. And then he winked, as if cake were an illicit substance and I'd find the offer irresistibly exciting. He waited expectantly.

'Let's go and see his house,' said Serge, coming to life. 'It can't do any harm.'

He turned to the little man. 'Cake, you say? Have you got any Ricard, by any chance?'

10

TINY TEARS

We followed the little man on foot through the shady avenue of poplar trees where the reek of Bruno's car exhaust still hung heavy in the air. Just before the main gate he turned off onto a weed-covered gravel path which led us along the boundary wall and up to a modest stone house with tiny shuttered windows and a small rounded wooden front door.

We stopped outside and evaluated the place, noting the missing tiles and stained and crumbling rendering. There was a plastic table surrounded by garden chairs out front and a small blow-up paddling pool with rubber ducks floating in the grassy water.

Serge caught my eye and pulled a face.

'My, what a sweet little place you have here!' he exclaimed melodramatically, holding his hands up in mock amazement. The shock of Bruno's unexpected betrayal seemed to have temporarily unbalanced him. He clapped his hands as if delighted.

'Yes, and I don't live all alone here either,' said the little man, oblivious to the irony. He felt in the pocket of his check trousers and produced an outsized key which he pushed into the keyhole in the little door.

He turned back to me and smiled. 'Now for that cake, eh?'

He swung back the door and stood aside for us to enter. I looked at Serge but he just shrugged, past caring. The little chap seemed harmless enough. He didn't look anything like my imagined profile of a serial killer. I threw caution to the wind and went in.

Inside it was dark and cold. I took a couple of steps and stopped, feeling around with my feet, afraid I might trip and fall headlong. I heard the little man go past me and the rattle of metal bolts. He threw back the shutters and the light streamed in.

As my eyes adjusted I saw we were standing in a long, low room that ran the whole length of the house. The walls were draped with an odd assortment of old bedspreads and rugs and the floor was covered in bright red lino. At the far end was a kitchenette with a sink, gas stove and Formica-topped table. He invited us to sit down at it while he busied himself boiling a saucepan of water and laying out plates, cups and saucers. He opened a cupboard and produced an octagonal tin box which he placed on the table. When the water boiled he spooned instant coffee and sugar into our cups and topped them up.

Serge looked disappointed. 'I believe there was some mention of Ricard. Is that not on the cards then?'

'I'm afraid not,' he said, opening the tin and taking out a large chocolate cake. The icing looked as if it had been put on with a builder's trowel.

'I made this myself,' he announced. 'I think you'll like it.'

He cut two large slices, placed them on our plates and stood watching us.

We sat silently staring at them.

'But you've got no Ricard?' said Serge.

'None, I'm sorry.'

'No wine or beer or anything like that?'

'No, nothing like that at all I'm afraid.'

'You're sure?'

'Absolutely.'

'Just this coffee and cake?'

'Yes.'

I took a sip of my coffee. 'Mmm, it's good,' I said.

The little man smiled, encouraged. He looked at Serge, waiting for his verdict.

'Bit hot for me,' said Serge. 'Would you have any cold water perhaps?'

The little man took his cup and went to the sink. While his back was turned Serge waved his forefinger in circles round his temple and gave me a tight grin. The bloke was bonkers.

I sipped at my coffee, looking round the room, postponing the moment when I was going to have to bite into my cake.

There was a bed in one corner. Perched in a line on it with their backs propped against the pillows were five or six dolls.

I hate dolls; cold, creepy monstrosities with their horrid pale faces and staring, beady little eyes. But I have been known to override my prejudice on discovering one that was worth a lot of money. These appeared to be old porcelain models dressed in their original faded costumes.

Serge had spotted them too. He got up, leaving his coffee and cake to have a look.

'Do you mind?' he said, picking one up.

'That's Anne Marie,' said the little man. He went over and took her carefully from Serge, replacing her gently back on the bed.

'She's been a naughty girl.'

'Has she now?' said Serge pulling another tight smile at me. 'My goodness, whatever next?' He picked up a second doll and lifted her hair, examining the back of her head. He pulled up her long embroidered cotton nightdress and inspected her naked private parts.

This appeared to greatly disturb the little man, who attempted to grab the doll back. As Serge lifted her high out of his reach his face contorted in extreme alarm and when Serge eventually handed her over he agitatedly smoothed down her nightdress, stroking her hair back into place and cuddling her up close.

I found this upsetting. There was something painfully sad about him living here all alone with just his dolls for company. We were imposing on his hospitality. Serge was taking liberties because he judged him to be a bit simple and I didn't like it.

'Come on, Serge, your coffee's getting cold,' I said. I took a bite of my cake and immediately wished I hadn't. It tasted strange with a musty under-taste that turned my stomach. I extricated the lump from my mouth and held it hidden under the table.

'I can't tell you how much I love these dolls of yours,' said Serge, ignoring me. 'They're very pretty indeed.'

The little guy was apprehensive now and nervous that Serge might start pulling them about again.

'They're resting just at the moment,' he said. 'They've been playing all morning and they need to calm down a bit.'

'Of course, of course,' said Serge, smiling what he thought was a reassuring smile, but which came out more like a leer.

'There are rather a lot of them though, aren't there? How do you cope with them all?'

The little man looked puzzled. 'They're no trouble at all,' he said. 'They're very good really.'

'Are they? Are they? Well, I'm pleased to hear it.' Serge leaned over again and picked up a third doll. 'Take this one, for instance...'

'Monique. That's Monique,' said the little man. He had his hands up ready to take her back and settle her down again. But Serge had her bent over on his arm examining the back of her head. He smoothed back the wig and beamed down at the little man.

'Yes, Monique. What a nice name. She's sweet isn't she? In fact she's just the sort of doll I'm looking for as a present for my little girl. It's her birthday tomorrow and I've not got her anything.'

The little man looked hurt and tears welled up in his eyes. 'Oh no, I couldn't possibly give her away. She lives here. This is her home.'

'I was thinking more of buying her really,' said Serge, unmoved. He pulled out what was left of his wad of euros and ran his fingers through it. 'Just think what you could do with all this money, and my little daughter would be so happy to have a lovely doll like this one for her birthday.'

The little guy looked pathetic. He was trapped with nowhere to turn.

'Come on, Serge,' I said. 'He doesn't want to sell any of his dolls. It's obvious they give him a lot of pleasure. Leave him alone, eh?'

Serge shot me a dagger look. He turned back to the little man.

'You've got several dolls here though, haven't you? Surely you could spare one for a sweet little girl?'

The bloke looked piteously towards me for help.

'Give it a rest, Serge,' I said. 'We've got a lot to do. We ought to get back to the chateau and finish loading up the stuff.'

'Sod the stuff!' Serge snapped at me. 'I'm talking to my little friend here and I'll thank you to stop interfering, Johnny.'

'I couldn't possibly part with any of my dollies,' said the little chap with a new determination. 'And I'd never sell them, I'm sorry.' My interruption seemed to have given him a chance to harden his resolve.

Serge looked thwarted, holding down his anger.

'No need to say never, eh? You might change your mind, you never know.'

The little man shook his head vigorously.

'Well, believe me, you might do. And if you do I'd like you to give me a ring. Would you do that for me?' He pulled his well-thumbed notebook out of his back pocket, jotted down his phone number, ripped out the sheet and handed it to him. The little man took it reluctantly.

'It's a nice place you've got,' I said, hoping to change the subject and lighten the mood. 'How long have you lived here then?'

'Oh, quite a few years now,' he said, coming over to me. 'The people who owned the chateau said I could move in here when my mother got very sick.'

'We've got to go now,' said Serge brusquely.

'But you can't yet, you've not finished your coffee and cake,' said the little man. 'Here I'll make you a *cadeau* of them.' He busied himself about in a drawer, produced two worn plastic bags and placed a piece of chocolate cake in each.

'Thank you, that's very kind,' said Serge taking his, rolling his eyes at me.

We reached the door and Serge stopped and looked around, smiling as if he'd been to a smashing party and had a lovely time.

'Now you won't forget what I told you, will you? If you need any money just give me a ring on that number.'

The little guy looked at him vacantly.

'Come on, let me hear you say it,' said Serge. 'Promise to ring me when you want to sell one of your little dollies. It would make my daughter so happy.'

He wasn't getting anywhere. The bloke was so obviously blanking the question that Serge gave up. We headed off down the path with him waving us goodbye. When we were out of his sight I let drop the squishy lump of my half-eaten cake and Serge lobbed his bag into the bushes.

'That bloody loony dwarf!' Serge spat out. 'He knows what those dolls are worth and he won't part with them.'

'You can hardly expect him to,' I said. 'They're all he's got in the world.'

'Do you know anything about dolls, Johnny?'

'Not really,' I said. 'I find them a bit creepy, that's all.'

'Yes, well, kindly don't try and lecture me then. I suppose you're aware, are you, that a couple of those dolls were made by Jumeau? They're French and the most desirable dolls you can get. Have you any idea what dolls like that are worth?'

'A lot?'

'Exactly, a hell of a lot. Like I said, they're wasted on a simpleton like him.'

When we got to the chateau Serge had completely lost interest in the rest of the contents. He couldn't even be bothered to fetch the hanging cane chair. He told the snaggle-toothed woman we'd be back another day and we drove off in an empty van.

A week later I bumped into Serge at a market and noticed immediately that he had a line of dolls perched at the back of his stand.

'You didn't, did you?' I said, shocked. 'You never went back and wheedled those dolls off that poor bloke?'

'No, those aren't his, Johnny,' he bridled. 'You've got it all wrong. I bought those dolls at auction this week.'

'Come on, Serge,' I said, not fooled. 'Those are that little man's dolls. I'd recognise them anywhere.'

He looked cornered for a moment and then realised he wasn't going to be able to dupe me. 'OK, Johnny, so they are the dwarf's dolls. You didn't want to know about them so I went back later and saw him again. I didn't steal them from him if that's what you're thinking. We came to an arrangement and he was fine about it.'

I was going to ask him what arrangement would make some poor sad little lonely man part with his most treasured possessions on earth, but realised I'd be wasting my breath and walked off.

For the rest of the day the poor little fellow and his dolls preyed on my mind. I felt I had to go back and see how he was.

Later that evening I drove out to the chateau, parked the van by the gate, followed the gravel path along the wall up to his house and knocked on his door.

There was no reply and the house was silent. I walked round the back and tried to see in the windows but the shutters were all bolted shut.

I was about to give up when he appeared unexpectedly, walking down the path, carrying an old duck's head umbrella.

'Hello,' I said. 'How are you? I was just passing through and thought I'd drop in. I hope you don't mind.'

He looked at me for a moment as if he wasn't sure who I was. Then his eyes lit up and he gave me a warm smile.

'So you're moving in at last?' he said. 'I'm so pleased.'

'I'm sorry, how do you mean?'

'You're one of the English people, aren't you? I'm so glad you're moving into the chateau at last. Do come in and have a cup of coffee and a piece of cake. I expect you're exhausted.'

The thought of his cake turned my stomach but I watched him unlock the door and accepted his invitation to come in and sit down. He switched on the lights and I immediately looked over towards the bed where his dolls had been. There was a line of dolls there still, but they weren't the delicate antiques with finely crafted porcelain faces of before. These dolls were big and shiny and made of plastic with bright painted faces and nylon wigs.

'I see you've got some different dolls,' I said.

'Yes, they're my new friends,' he said excitedly. 'We've been having *such* fun together.'

So Serge had managed to persuade him to exchange his valuable old dolls for new, worthless, plastic shiny ones.

Unbelievable! The old bugger was incorrigible.

But still... he didn't seem at all perturbed. In fact he almost seemed to prefer his new dolls.

He poured me a coffee and I knocked it back but passed on the cake, politely refusing his offer to bag a piece to take with me.

As I drove home I couldn't help marvelling at Serge's tenacity. Once he'd seen those dolls he wasn't going to give up till he'd got them. But it was essentially a rotten trick. It was just about as low as he could possibly stoop. I was wrong about that, as it turned out. He could stoop a lot lower.

11

DUBIOUS ARTS

It was the end of January. The night air was chill and clear, and a fat full moon floated in a sky choked with stars. I'd bumped into Serge after Christmas when money was tight and he'd persuaded me that I needed to try a pitch at St Michelle Market in Bordeaux.

'I've been doing it off and on for years,' he said. 'It's good fun and I'll introduce you to a few of my mates up there.'

Over the past three months I'd not seen much of Serge and had more or less forgiven him for his trick with the dolls. It had been a quiet winter and I needed to work.

'You have to get there on Saturday night and sleep in the van,' he said. 'Then you can be up bright and early and bag a place.

St Michelle is in the old poor quarter of the city. As I drove alongside the river I could see the distinctive floodlit spire of Saint Michelle Church standing over the city. The heater was blasting out but I could still feel the bite of the cold air outside seeping in round the door. I wasn't relishing the idea of a night in the van when I could be at home tucked up in bed with Helen.

The tyres bounced over the cobblestones as I circumnavigated a concrete-posted wall searching for an entrance between iron bollards. I found one, drove onto the square, parked, and pulled on my woollen hat and gloves. Serge had told me to meet him in the cafe so I headed towards the nearest one.

There was someone lying on his back on the pavement. I assumed it was a drunk, but as I drew closer I saw it was Serge, arms and legs out like St Andrew on the cross. He was flat out on a large iron grill set in the cobblestones. When he saw it was me he stuck out his gloved hand to be shaken. I bent over and felt a rush of hot air from below.

He patted the grill. It was like sitting on a convector heater.

He clapped and whooped with delight. 'It's from the subway. If you park your van here you'll be warm as toast.'

A young couple, arms round each other, stopped to look down on us. When they felt the warm air they stepped out onto the grill. Serge gave me a nudge as the warm air lifted the girl's skirt.

'Your girlfriend has pretty legs and lingerie,' said Serge, 'you lucky sod.'

The young man laughed and he and his girl went off arm in arm.

'See, you stick with me and we'll see some sights. You hungry, Johnny? Come on, let's go eat.'

St Michelle was hopping at this hour of a Saturday night. The restaurants and bars were packed to overflowing. We hurried through the cobbled streets; past neon-lit cafes full of neatly suited young Arabs; through an empty, silent market bestrewn with rotting fruit and broken cardboard boxes; down a dark alleyway and up a short cul-de-sac to an anonymous-looking doorway.

'Eh, hold on to your hat, British, this is it – the Portuguese restaurant I told you about.'

He went to push open the door, but it was jammed. He barged into it and forced his way through the heaving mass of bodies until we were pressed up against a bar where customers were quaffing beers and aperitifs waiting for a table.

Serge was clearly well known here. Half-cut characters full of the joys of Saturday night pushed forward to wring his hand and slap him on the back. I was introduced as *'mon ami l'Anglais'* and my hand was wrung and my back slapped as well. Although Bordeaux has its fair share of English inhabitants they didn't appear to be much in evidence in this bar.

'I've heard you have to stand on a box to say what you want in England – is this true?' a big grizzle-haired man with a huge pot belly asked me.

I realised he must be talking about Speaker's Corner in Hyde Park and assured him it wasn't compulsory.

'But you can't say just what you like about the Queen.'

I nodded, agreeing with him. It was probably quicker.

'You English are buying up France bit by bit. There's even English mayors in some villages full of Englishmen. Is that right, I ask you? Is that right?'

'Certainly not,' I said, trying to edge away.

'But at least it's better than being taken over by the whoring Germans... or the Dutch. The Dutch bring all their own food with them when they come here. What's wrong with French food, that's what I'd like to know. It's the best in the world.' I agreed with him and backed off.

'The Dordogne is full of English and Germans now,' he went on. 'Some of those Germans even own chateaux there. They wiped out whole villages during the war and now we let them walk in and buy up all our historical buildings. It's a crime.'

I looked about frantically, trying to escape from the xenophobic bore.

Serge was up at the bar deep in conversation with a swarthy character with curly brown hair and a bright blue scarf tied round his neck.

Serge waved me over. 'This is my good friend Jesus,' he said. 'Jesus Raines – ask anybody, he's famous.' He gave me a tight smile. 'He's a musician like you, so you two should get on.'

When the guy shook my hand the skin felt lumpy, and when he turned I saw livid white scar tissue running from under the blue scarf and up the side of his face.

'He's a fantastic Flamenco guitarist, but can't play any more,' said Serge. He reached down and lifted Jesus' hand. It was scarred and bent crooked like a crow's foot.

'My caravan caught fire and I was burnt,' said Jesus almost apologetically. 'I was asleep and didn't wake up.'

Serge was miming at me over his shoulder the familiar French boozer sign, thumb pointing at his mouth indicating a large intake of alcohol.

'My wife and two of my children died,' he said mechanically, as if his emotions were cut off.

'But you still have your son Buddy,' said Serge, as usual looking for the silver lining. 'And my God, you should hear him play, Johnny. He taught him everything he knows… He's a credit to him.'

Jesus brightened at this and seemed to come back to life.

'That's true, and he plays better than I ever did.'

Serge shook his head and pulled a face at me over his shoulder as if to say 'no way'.

'He tours all over Europe and is frequently on television,' said Jesus. 'He lives in Paris now.'

'You must eat with us,' said Serge. 'You can tell Johnny all about your son.' He slammed his hand down hard on the wooden counter top.

'Eh, Didier, what about our table? We got to wait till we're too weak to lift our knives and forks?'

The barman in a blue apron shrugged. 'You'll have to take your turn with everyone else, Serge.' He waved his hands over the crowded room. 'Everyone's hungry but are they complaining?'

A tough, gaunt man with grey hair tied back in a ponytail and silver earrings came pushing his way through. He put his arms around Serge from behind and hugged him tight.

Serge twisted round annoyed, but when he saw who it was he was delighted.

'Eh, Marcel, you son of a cheap whore, I thought it was the DST caught up with me at last.' He screamed with laughter and pumped the bloke's hand, slapping him on the back. The DST (Direction de la Surveillance du Territoire) is the French equivalent of MI5.

'Eh, Johnny, meet Marcel the Lyonnaise. If you want to know anything about French antiques, he's the bloke to ask.'

The guy gave me a wink, felt about in his denim jacket pocket and produced a small leather-bound book which he handed to me. 'Go on, have a look at that.'

I opened it carefully. It was obviously very old, engraved on a kind of yellowed parchment paper.

The title page read, *'L'Art de Péter – Theori – Physyque et Méthodique'*.

I glanced up. 'Go on, feast your eyes – you'll never see another book like it.' He was gleeful.

I turned the pages carefully. All the 'S's were written as 'F's and my ancient French wasn't up to much so it was difficult to decipher. There were old illustrations on *'L'Art de Péter'*; comical little figures bent over chairs, trousers round their ankles emitting puffs of smoke from their anuses. Pages of script explaining the secrets of farting. Until finally – presumably after studying the book closely – *'On peut péter avec règle et avec goût.'* (One can break wind with control and with taste.)

The book appeared to be the nineteenth-century precursor to *Viz*'s Johnny Fartipants. The last time I'd really laughed at breaking wind was when I first saw the Mel Brooke's film *Blazing Saddles*. It was one of those taboos that had been well and truly broken and now only afforded me the occasional chuckle. But I was familiar with the French love of Le Petomaine, the great master of controlled farting who wowed Paris at the beginning of the twentieth century. It was amusing to see an antique book like this devoted to the art and I didn't have to try very hard to express the amused amazement that was clearly expected of me. It was like reading Chaucer's *The Miller's Tale* for the first time, bringing home the simple truth that rude noises from the bottom had been making mankind laugh for centuries.

I shut it and went to hand it back but Serge snatched it away and began waving it in the air.

'Have you any idea of the value of this thing, Johnny?' His eyes were wide with disbelief. He began to turn the pages, examining them with reverence. 'You swine, Marcel, where in the name of the Holy Mother of God did you find this little gem?'

Marcel tapped the side of his nose with his forefinger. 'Aha, wouldn't you like to know. I can't say. It's a secret.'

'Secret, my arse! You stole this book, you must have.'

'Let's say I acquired it through legitimate channels,' said Marcel, taking it back and replacing it carefully in his denim jacket pocket.

'How much do you want for it?' said Serge.

'You think you can afford to buy this? You're dreaming, my friend. I'll wait for the right buyer. This book is a three-month holiday for me lying on soft sandy beaches sipping exotic cocktails surrounded by beautiful women. You think I'll give it to you at a knock-down price?' He snorted.

The waitress came over to tell us she'd found us a place.

'Come and eat with us, Marcel,' said Serge. 'We'll have a laugh.'

'OK, I won't eat with you, but I'll drink your wine as I aim to get out of it and sleep deeply in my van on such a cold night.'

'But if you wake up shivering,' said Serge, 'don't come creeping round in the early hours wanting me to warm you up.' He found his own joke hilarious and was still chuckling as we seated ourselves at a long table elbow to elbow with other diners.

Jesus joined us and sat next to me. He produced a small bottle of Spanish brandy from his coat pocket, emptied it into a wine glass, took a big swig and pulled a face.

'My medicine,' he said grimly.

A large tureen was plonked in front of us and Serge ladled out spoonfuls of soup into my bowl. It was green and gelatinous, with cabbage leaves, peas and other unidentifiable vegetables floating about in it. I tasted it gingerly. It was delicious.

Serge grabbed a handful of cut country bread from a basket and handed me a thick slice. 'Eh, come on, British, get stuck in. We've got big helpings to get through.'

Marcel reached for an unlabelled bottle of red wine, filled his glass and knocked it back in one go.

'A good year, is it?' said Serge, winking at me.

'This soup's not bad, Marcel.' He went to ladle some in his bowl but Marcel held his hand over it. 'No, none for me, Serge, I told you. I want to get legless and pass out in the van.'

'You need something warm inside you on a night like this,' insisted Serge. 'Take a bit of soup. It'll do you good.'

'I'll maybe have some chicken later,' said Marcel. He poured wine into our glasses and topped up his own.

The soup plates were cleared. Serge had ordered me salted cod. 'It's a traditional Portuguese dish, absolutely delicious.'

It arrived on a large oval dish in a thick sauce. When I tasted it the sheer saltiness of it almost made me gag.

'See, what did I tell you? It's a lot better than what you get in England, isn't it? I've been to your country and let's be fair, the food is not good.'

I tried to force down the fish in small bits with lumps of bread and gulps of wine to take away the salty taste. If I didn't watch it I'd be falling off the wagon. But I reasoned that a few sips of wine wouldn't do any harm.

'Eh, you wouldn't believe it,' said Marcel, waving his glass in the air. 'I had those EDF electricity people around my place yesterday trying to tell me I've got to let them connect me up.'

'Marcel lives miles away from anyone, deep in the forest,' Serge explained. 'You don't believe in electricity, do you, Marcel?'

'You're damn right I don't. I hate the stuff. Who needs it? When it gets dark you go to bed, when it gets light you get up – end of story. I'm not paying their fancy prices for something I don't use.'

'You don't have a radio or TV?' I asked.

He pulled a face full of scorn. 'What would I need them for? They're rubbish.'

I was inclined to agree with him. He had a point.

'On dark winter evenings I light my oil lamp, sit by the warm stove and read a good book. What could be better than that, I'd like to know? They're worried that my way of life could catch on and then where would they be if people start to realise they don't need their damned electricity?'

Serge tapped my plate with his fork. 'If you don't want that cod, Johnny, give it to me. I love it.'

I admitted it had beaten me. He scraped it onto his plate and piled on a mound of boiled potatoes. 'My advice is never pass up on good food; you never know where the next meal's coming from.'

The waitress brought us a selection of sickly sweet cakes on a silver dish, which we ate with liqueurs followed by chocolate mousse and small cups of extremely strong coffee. The restaurant was beginning to empty. We paid our bill and staggered out the door.

The air was so cold it took my breath away. We walked unsteadily back to the square and when I tried the lock of my van it was frozen solid. Serge warmed my key with his cigarette lighter and after a couple of tries it opened.

'Have you got enough blankets and stuff there, Johnny?' he asked.

I assured him I had two sleeping bags and plenty of blankets and after bidding him and Marcel goodnight I climbed up into the front of my van.

Serge rapped on the window. 'Don't forget, you have to wake up and unload at four or someone else will bag your place.'

I assured him I understood and began to arrange my bed. I laid a plank of wood I had specially for this purpose across the two front seats and covered it with cushions. I took off my boots and climbed into one sleeping bag and then wriggled into the other, pulling the hood over my head and tying it tight.

I lay back and tried to relax, hearing the sound of cars starting up and roaring off; the voices of late-night revellers straggling across the square; muffled disco music from a nearby cafe. After a couple of minutes my nose began to freeze. I pulled my woolly hat over the front of my face and tied the hood even tighter. The rest of me was warm enough in my two sleeping bags and I must have fallen deeply asleep because I was woken by frantic banging. A gloved hand was scraping away the ice on the window and Serge's face appeared in the hole.

'Wake up, Johnny. Something terrible's happened – a catastrophe!' He was distraught.

I struggled out of my sleeping bags, pulled on my coat and gloves and lurched after him across the icy square to a parked white van nearby. He opened the front door and drew back a blanket to reveal Marcel the Lyonnaise. His face was white and waxy with a bluish tinge, starkly lit by an overhead street light.

'I can't wake him,' he said. 'I've tried everything. He's as cold as stone. I think maybe...' His voice cracked. 'I think maybe he's frozen to death.'

I'd been laughing with Marcel a couple of hours ago. It didn't seem possible. Was Serge playing a joke on me?

'Perhaps he's not dead,' I said. I pinched his cheek. It was icy.

'Have you phoned for an ambulance?'

'I've done it – on the mobile. They should be here any moment.'

As he spoke I heard the *whoop-whoop* of a siren and saw flashing red lights. A white ambulance marked 'SAMU' with big black letters on the side was coming across the square. Serge ran towards it, waving his hands about, pointing the driver towards the van.

Two men in dayglo jackets leaped out and began trying to revive Marcel. One of them turned to us and shook his head.

'He's gone, I'm afraid. Do you know who he is? Was he a friend of yours?'

Serge explained. They took his address and phone number.

'The gendarmes should be round later to take a statement from you both.' They examined Marcel's identity card. 'He was only forty-two,' said one of them. 'He looks a lot older.'

'He lived a life, that one,' said Serge ruefully. 'He crammed a lot into the years.'

'He most probably had a heart attack or died of hypothermia,' said the ambulance driver. They lifted his body into the back of the ambulance and drove off.

Lorries and white vans were starting to arrive in the square.

Heavy pieces of antique furniture were being unloaded, trestle tables erected. There were shouts of greeting and excited chatter.

'I can't believe it,' said Serge. 'Why Marcel? He was always so strong. How could he just die like this?' He pushed his gloved hands deep in his pockets to warm them up. Then he pulled something out and turned it over. I recognised Marcel's little leather-bound book, *L'Art de Péter*.

My face must have given me away because Serge reacted. 'What? Don't look at me like that, Johnny. What was I supposed to do? If I'd left it on the body someone else would only have stolen it. Marcel's got no use for it now. He'd have wanted me to have it.'

I didn't say anything.

'A dead man can't take a three-month holiday lying on soft sandy beaches sipping exotic cocktails surrounded by beautiful women.' He shrugged his shoulders. 'But I can.'

Two young dealers unloading a massive armoire from the back of a lorry shouted across a greeting to us. 'How's it going, Serge? Cold enough for you?'

'You won't say anything, will you, Johnny? You know, about me taking Marcel's little book?'

What could I say? He was giving me his pathetic innocent little boy look.

'No, Serge,' I said. 'Don't worry, I won't breathe a word.'

12

PARASOLS AND HARMONICAS

The ancient city of Bayonne looked uncannily like a stage set at this early hour of the morning; two-dimensional cardboard cut-out stone walls, backlit by the soft red glow of the rising sun. It was surprisingly warm and a dry Spanish wind was blowing in from across the Pyrenees, rustling the leaves on the Platanes. The medieval streets and alleyways that run back into the old town appeared darkly menacing as if hooded fiends lurked in the shadows. Bayonne is the nearest big town to us, an hour's drive down the motorway towards the Spanish border.

The Ramparts at Bayonne are all that remain of the high stone walls that were built to fortify the town by the Marquis de Vauban, the military genius who supervised the fortifications of major cities all over France, in the seventeenth century. Bayonne has a bellicose history and purportedly the bayonet was invented here. When I walked to the edge and looked down from the top of the walls into the gloom I could imagine an invading army scaling rickety ladders while the townsfolk poured hot oil on their heads from colossal cast iron cauldrons.

It was the beginning of April and the *brocante* markets were beginning to come alive again after a quiet winter. Happily, winter here in south-west France is normally a short one. Sometimes the weather can be hot and sunny right up to Christmas Day and then after two or three months of comparative cold it often begins to warm up again.

I was here on Serge's advice to take part in the first of what was hoped would be a regular market on the walkway that runs along the top of the old city walls.

'It's strange that no one runs a regular market in Bayonne,' he'd told me. 'You know my *copain*, Stefan?'

I did, actually. I'd met him a few times and talked about music. He was a big blues fan.

'Well, he's got permission from the *mairie* so don't miss the opportunity to get a pitch. *Premier levé, premier servi.*' (The early bird catches the worm.)

A knot of *brocanteurs* were huddled together, cigarette ends glowing, and as I approached I could hear Serge holding forth.

'It's no good going on at me. It's not my fault he's not here. He's probably still in bed with one of his mistresses. How should I know? Look, just set up your stands and we'll sort it all out later.'

The small crowd began to disperse, grumbling. When Serge spotted me, he came over and shook my hand.

'Eh, Johnny, hear that did you? What a bunch of moaners.'

'Problem?' I said.

'No, it's just Stefan, he's always late, the lazy sod. Grab a place and get set up. It looks like it could be a free-for-all.'

I went back to my van and was manoeuvring it into what I considered a good spot when Serge came over, arms waving.

'Hey, Johnny, not there. Come over next to me by the snack stand. It's the best pitch on the market.' He guided me into position and I began to unpack my stuff.

Like all the itinerant traders in France I carried a giant parasol for protection against the elements. It's the parasols that give the markets their colourful continental character. That and the habit the town councils have of relaying cheerful music from small loudspeakers cunningly positioned about the towns.

I parked and began unloading the gear, hefting the heavy metal stand of the parasol onto the walkway on top of the wall. I splayed the feet, secured it with the locking screw and went to fetch the umbrella part which I inserted into the base and opened. It was four metres long by three metres wide, covered in cheerful red canvas with yellow stripes and scalloped edging. It's actually the most important piece of equipment in the *brocanteur*'s arsenal. Your parasol gives shelter from the sun when it sizzles, and from the rain when it drizzles. In a downpour you can fasten special plastic sides all round as protection from the driving rain. Without your parasol you're at the mercy of the elements and you grow to depend on it never letting you down.

I sniffed the air. It smelled like it might rain. There was no moon; the sky to the west was still dark and I was unable to pick out any cloud formations. Working outside I had grown accustomed to watching the sky, predicting oncoming storms and bad weather. But the air was still. Even so it might be wise to secure the four corners of the parasol, just in case. I had seen people being led away with blood running down their faces from nasty flesh wounds caused by the metal spokes of an out-of-control parasol blown by the wind.

I was feeling about in the back of the van for the weights and cords to secure mine when there was the roar of a powerful motorbike and Stefan turned up on his big black Harley-Davidson.

'Eh, Johnny, how's it going?' He cut the engine and climbed off to shake my hand. Although his mother was French his German father had bequeathed him a six-foot frame, sandy blond hair and an easy sense of his own superiority. He stood at least a head and shoulders above most of the locals.

'What time do you call this?' said Serge. 'I nearly had a riot on my hands earlier.'

Stefan's eyes were twinkling. 'My new girlfriend held me hostage in bed this morning. You wouldn't want me to disappoint her, would you, Serge?'

He turned to me. 'I'm hoping you have brought your harmonicas with you, Johnny. I fancy some down home blues at lunchtime.'

I was about to reply but my eyes were drawn to something moving overhead. Aliens were landing at Bayonne!

A giant shadow with a twinkling undercarriage was hovering high above us. I watched hypnotised as the huge ship twisted and turned, searching for a suitable place to land.

Serge gave a yell and threw himself forward into the back of my van.

I looked again and realised with a rush of fear and perfect clarity that this was no alien spaceship, but my parasol. I recognised the crucifix shape of the heavy metal base. Strong winds had swept it up the edge of the Ramparts and carried it silently high into the air like a piece of thistle down. The legends of stallholders being carried off like Mary Poppins on their umbrellas suddenly didn't seem so far-fetched.

I instinctively raised my arms to protect myself, expecting it to crash down on us. But it gave a sudden twist and floated off over the road towards the headlights of an oncoming car.

I watched, mesmerised, holding my breath. If it dropped now and the heavy metal base went through the windscreen there was a strong possibility the driver would be killed or badly injured. In that split second I was wondering if our *responsabilité civile* insurance would cover such an eventuality.

It plummeted down and crashed onto the car bonnet, bouncing off, spraying bright sparks as the metal base hit the road. The car skidded to a halt and the driver climbed out, looking shocked. I rushed to calm him. He bent over to examine the ugly dent in his car bonnet and looked at me, nonplussed. We both watched Stefan sprint past, chasing after the umbrella that was being dragged along the road.

'I'm really sorry,' I said. 'The wind.'

There was a blinding flash of lightning followed by a rumble of thunder.

Stefan had caught up with the umbrella. The canvas was torn and the frame was bent. He held it aloft, grinning.

The man took hold of my sleeve. 'My car... what about my car?' He looked as though he was having difficulty dealing with all this before his *petit-déjeuner*.

There was a queue of traffic forming. Serge was out in the middle of the road directing it. Someone got out to see what was happening. A horn sounded. I persuaded the driver of the damaged car to pull over and gave him my insurance details. I only hoped I was covered.

'I never expected to be bombed from the air like that,' he said. 'It's not the sort of thing that happens in Bayonne.'

As he drove off there was a deafening clap of thunder and the heavens opened. I joined Serge and Stefan, who were sheltering in the back of my van. We watched the water swirling in the gutter, carrying a debris of twigs and fallen leaves.

'Lucky that bloke wasn't killed, eh, Johnny?' said Serge.

'It was a miracle,' I sighed.

'Your umbrella's not too bad,' Stefan pointed out. 'You'll be able to fix it. Next time make sure it's tied down. You have to take precautions when you put it up, just the same as with women.' He gave a filthy laugh.

The rain was easing off. The early morning sky began to brighten and the bank of black clouds rolled back to reveal blue skies. I felt upset about my damaged parasol, but probably not as shaken as the poor bloke who almost got killed by it.

Serge reassured me. 'Don't worry, Johnny, I've got some sticky tape to fix the holes in your parasol. It'll be as good as new.'

I remembered how his parasol had various taped crosses positioned all over it. Now I knew how they got there.

'I don't think we'll see much more rain,' said Stefan. 'You can leave your van parked where it is next to Serge.

A big fat jolly character known as Pepé Le Frite who ran the snacks stand was sweating profusely as he unloaded boxes of *saucissons et frites* (sausages and chips) ready for the lunchtime rush.

When I went back to my van to fetch the rest of the gear a weaselly bloke wearing a fifties-style blue mohair thug's coat and polished black brogues was overseeing three moots (who could all have found jobs as extras in a gangster movie) unloading Turkish carpets and reproduction furniture from a white Iveco van double-parked in the road. He came over when he saw me open my van doors.

'Eh! You can't park there.' Up close I could see he had a sinister moustache. It was like a shadow, shaved close and bristly. The three burly blokes put down the wardrobe they were carrying and watched.

'That's our place. Better shift it if you know what's good for you.'

'I don't think so, this is the first one,' I said. 'And I was allocated this spot.'

He looked at me like I was an insignificant piece of dirt. He had the air of someone who wasn't used to being ignored.

All the spaces on the road were full. If I did as he said, I would have to drive to the car park that was right up the other end. I looked around in vain for Stefan or Serge.

'Eh, you deaf or something? Shift that van.' The three moots, who looked like brothers, began to stroll over. Their faces were eager, as if they could smell a ruck.

'The organiser told me I could leave my van here,' I said weakly. 'Look, I'm stalled out just over there.' I waved towards the snacks stand.

'I don't give a shit, that's our place. Move it.'

The three moots were looking at me over his shoulder like I was a piece of squashed dog's crap.

There was a time when I was younger and more reckless in England when I would have taken great exception to being ordered about by a bully like this. But now I was weighing up whether I should simply capitulate and park somewhere else, or stand up to them. I didn't fancy my chances and although resorting to physical violence was generally considered a weakness in France I had witnessed enough *bagarres* (punch-ups) to know that these three were capable of flying in the face of fashion.

The weaselly bloke came up close. His breath smelled terrible and for a second I thought he was going to bite me.

'Where you from, Chef? Only you've got a bit of a funny accent.'

'England,' I said. 'I'm English.'

'Really, is that right? Well, listen here, English, do you understand what I'm saying?'

'Yes,' I said.

'You sure? Because I don't want anyone to say later I didn't give you a chance.'

I nodded. I didn't like the way things were going. I began to feel around in my pockets for the van keys. I was loath to back down, but four against one didn't seem like very good odds.

The three moots were shaking their heads and grinning at each other. It was obvious I was about to capitulate.

'Do you know Stefan, the bloke who runs the market here?' I said, playing for time.

The weaselly bloke with the moustache looked like he couldn't believe I was still bothering to show any resistance. He was poised on the balls of his feet as if about to fell me with a short sharp jab to the jaw.

'I was actually told I could park here,' I said.

The bloke's eyes widened. He was near the end of his tether.

'OK, I'll shift it,' I said. It wasn't worth getting a busted jaw over. Broken bones took time to heal and I couldn't afford to be laid off over something so trivial.

I climbed into the van and started the engine.

'Eh, Johnny, are you leaving?' It was Serge, appearing in the nick of time.

'The *rosbif* is off back to England,' said the Weasel.

The three moots laughed and slapped each other's backs. They obviously thought this was the funniest thing they'd ever heard.

Serge was about to step in when Stefan appeared.

He looked at the Weasel and his cronies and appeared to grasp what was happening straight away.

'Stay where you are, John.' He turned on the Weasel.

'I told him he could leave his van there. You're going to have to take yours up the car park.'

The Weasel looked like he couldn't believe what he was hearing. He threw Stefan a look that would have shrivelled a less confident man.

Stefan went up to the three moots. 'Unload your stuff and get your van up the car park.' They were still grinning inanely, not quite sure what was happening.

Stefan beckoned the Weasel over. 'Any more trouble and I'll see to it you never work this market again.'

The Weasel looked at the Turkish carpets and all the repro furniture they had unloaded and I could almost hear his brain calculating if it was worth sacrificing a day's takings just to make a point. He decided it wasn't and grudgingly gave orders to the moots to finish unloading and park the van.

As I unloaded the rest of my stuff the four of them watched me, eyes ablaze. When I passed the Weasel, he spat out, 'Don't think you've got away with this, English, I don't forget people who cross me.'

I tried to ignore him and get on with setting up, but I felt sick to my stomach.

Serge sidled over from his stand.

'I don't like to tell you this, Johnny, but that's the Sanchez mob. We'd better watch out. They're a bunch of gangsters, that lot. Even the police are scared of them.'

Great! That's just what I wanted to hear. I'd been coming to terms with the problem and now one remark from Serge had me shitting myself again. So that Weasel bloke meant what he said, and I couldn't rely on Stefan or Serge to protect me.

Manuel, a Manouche Gypsy I knew from previous markets, and who was stalled out nearby, came across for a quiet word.

'Eh, John, I saw what happened there. Pity you upset that guy. All the *gitans* say he's a troublemaker. He's bad news, I'm afraid.'

Gulp! Everyone knew about them except me. I thanked him for the tip-off and wished I'd been forewarned. I appeared to have made a dangerous enemy.

For the rest of the morning I waited with some trepidation for the third stroke of bad luck to strike. But the wet weather held off and crowds of people turned up to stroll along the Ramparts and check out what the *brocante* market had to offer. The music from a wind-up gramophone floated up from the far end across the stalls. People were smiling and laughing. The good citizens of Bayonne appeared in high spirits, determined to enjoy their Saturday morning.

I perked up a bit when I had the good fortune to sell a nineteenth-century Meerschaum pipe in the shape of a nymph's head to a collector who was well pleased with his purchase. We had discovered that French collectors of these pipes, which are carved by hand from a soft stone reported to be solidified sea foam, had difficulties in finding examples in good condition and Helen had bought this one at an auction in England. Those featuring the scantily clad figures of women appeared to be extremely popular as most customers were men. As he paid me cash in large denomination notes I caught sight of the Weasel out of the corner of my eye, watching us. When he saw I'd seen him he gave a sneer and turned away.

In the rush before noon I managed to forget about him and his intimidating threats. Pepé Le Frite had his charcoal burner going full steam and I was overpowered by the pungent aroma of *saucissons* sizzling on the grill and the hiss of chips in the deep fat fryer.

Serge was at the front of the queue. He shouted across to me to join him.

Pepé handed him a greasy sausage in a baguette, and wanted to know what I wanted. There wasn't a lot of choice. It was either *saucissons* or a thick slice of Brie cheese wedged in a baguette, an unappetising snack at the best of times. I decided to settle for that and reached out to take one.

'Free cup of wine with that,' said Pepé. Before I could stop him he held a paper cup up to a giant brown plastic barrel and twisted the tap, letting a stream of bright red liquid splash into it.

'Eh, Johnny, don't touch that muck,' said Serge. 'It'll burn your insides out.'

Pepé looked wounded and speared a couple of sausages to cover his hurt feelings.

'We'll open this bottle of Bordeaux instead, much better for the digestion.'

Stefan called us over to join him at his table. They uncorked the wine and insisted I have a glass. I didn't want to appear rude and refuse their hospitality. Whenever I told any of the market people I was an alcoholic the response was normally, 'So am I, what of it?' followed by a swift downing of the glass they were holding. If truth be told, I was still a bit shaken from the confrontation with the Weasel and his cronies and this had weakened my normal resolve.

Halfway through the meal another bottle was produced and after quaffing back several more glassfuls Stefan insisted I get out my harmonicas and sing them some 'low down blues'. With my inhibitions considerably lowered I launched into a spirited version of Sonny Boy Williamson's 'Bring It on Home', to loud shouts of encouragement. This was followed – at Serge's insistence – by John Lee Hooker's 'Boom-Boom'. And he joined in all the choruses, yelling out the 'Boom-Boom-Boom-Boom's, and banging his plate randomly with his knife and fork.

I needed something in my stomach to counteract the effect of the wine, but when I reached for my baguette I realised Serge Bastarde had eaten it.

'Sorry, Johnny, I wasn't thinking,' he said. He offered to get me another.

Sitting back for a breather I noticed the Weasel and his three moots had moved in closer. They were sitting on a shiny repro Louis XV sofa watching what was going on. It made the hairs on the back of my neck prickle.

After coffees, on my way back to the van, slightly tipsy and in need of a siesta, I had to pass close by them. They watched me approach and the Weasel got up and stood in my path waiting for me.

He was blocking my way. And my heart sank further when the three moots joined him shoulder to shoulder on the pavement.

Surely they weren't going to give me a good kicking in broad daylight? They'd never get away with it. If I was in trouble, Stefan and Serge would help out. But when I glanced round to check I saw them disappearing up the other end of the market.

As I drew level the Weasel stepped towards me and when he raised his arm I flinched, thinking he was about to attack. But to my surprise he embraced me and slapped me on the back.

'Eh, Harmonica!' He grinned in my face and shook my hand.

I must have looked shocked because he said it again.

'Eh, Harmonica!' He gave my hand an extra squeeze. 'The blues. Very good.'

All our previous problems were forgotten. He was now my biggest buddy. The three moots joined in, beaming and patting me on the back.

I walked on to my van with a feeling of relief flooding over me. And as I settled down on the front seat I could see the Weasel smiling and giving me the thumbs-up sign. I waved and smiled back. I was worried that I might have fallen off the wagon but relieved that I'd won the Weasel over. The world of *brocanteurs* was comparatively small and I didn't need to make any enemies.

As I drifted into an alcoholic stupor I was thinking to myself... it's true what that bloke said... Music doth have charms to soothe the savage beast... Or breast... Or whatever it was.

13

CORSETS AND COQUETTES

The mournful hooting of owls greeted me as I stepped out of the house into a nightscape lit by a crimson moon. It hung enormous over the trees, so close I could have reached out and touched it. It was four in the morning in the middle of June and I had a three-hour drive ahead. I was off to a weekend antiques market held twice a year in a little town deep in the heart of the Gironde.

I closed the shuttered doors quietly behind me. I didn't want to wake Helen, who was tucked up fast asleep in bed. The pigeons in their boxes under the eaves cooed inquisitively at one another and the big fat toad who lives in the yard crawled off as I walked over to my van.

The single-track road that passes the end of our drive snakes over small hills through dense deciduous woodland interspersed with open arable land. Most of the Landes is flat and sandy and covered with pine forests, but this comparatively unknown area a few kilometres inland with its rolling hills and small farms is known as the Chalosse. As I rounded a bend I was confronted by a pair of small deer caught in the headlights. The French call them *chevreuils*, and with their delicate bodies and short pointed horns they could have jumped straight off one of the old Babycham champagne perry bottles.

I braked and extinguished my lights. It was a doe with her fawn, and I watched in the moonlight as she waited to make sure her youngster was well into the thicket at the side of the road before unhurriedly following her in.

I drove on, thrilled with the memory of what I had just witnessed. In the distance blue lights were flashing, and as I descended the hill that leads into our local village I could see a cluster of vehicles pulled off the road. A gendarme with a torch waved me down. Firemen were bent over a saloon car which had careered down a steep embankment and into a tree. In the headlights I saw the back end of a red Ford Escort with its 'go faster' stripes that I thought might belong to the son of one our local farmers. A young girl with blood streaming down her face was being helped into an ambulance.

The gendarme with the torch spoke to me. 'Nasty business. Seems like a young couple were on their way home with friends from the disco. The girl had a miraculous escape.'

'What about the others?' I asked. He shook his head. 'They're trying to cut them out now, but it's not good.'

I asked if there was anything I could do.

'Not really. We've phoned his family. It's up to the cutting crew and medics now.'

I drove on for a while and then pulled over, got out and leaned against the side of my van, feeling shaky. I was used to coming across crashed cars in the early hours of Saturday or Sunday morning on my way to markets. They more often than not involved young drivers who had over-imbibed at the local *boîte de nuit* (disco). But this one had been a bit close to home.

On the other side of the village I picked up the dual carriageway and after a half-hour run turned off onto the Route National that runs through the forest. The only cars I had passed had been a few stragglers wending their way home from 'Le Soft' nightclub. But now, driving through the dense pine forests, the roads were deserted. My mind was turning as it tended to do at this early hour of the morning, mulling over the past, wondering about the future. The accident had shaken me up and I was re-evaluating my place in the world.

I was also slightly neurotically keeping an eye out for any stray deer that might jump out onto the road ahead. Startling stories appeared regularly in the local section of the *Sud Ouest* newspaper about motorists who had crashed off the road trying to avoid hitting *chevreuils*. Our village shop even sold small patented plastic whistling devices to fix on the outside of your car designed to scare off any deer that might be thinking of leaping out. It was a handy excuse for any motorist who lost control of his vehicle on the way home after one too many at the neighbourhood bar, so most reports of the phenomenon tended to be anecdotal.

I kept looking at my Michelin map, checking I was on the right road. Helen had booked up with the fair organisers in advance and all I had to do was turn up early to set up. It was the first time I had done a market here so it was new territory for me. Despite their habit of accenting the importance of living the good life I had noticed the French tended to work hard, starting the day at a ridiculously early hour and continuing until quite late. The art was to make it look like you were really enjoying yourself and not working hard at all.

The misty dawn light brightened as I left the forest and turned off onto a series of smaller roads winding through sleepy villages. There were thin blue lines denoting small rivers on the map and the village I was headed for appeared to be situated among them. I carried on down a tiny road with wide ditches and swathes of bulrushes on either side. I ignored a temporary sign by the side of the road warning of 'Inondation' or flooding. I had long since adopted the French habit of disregarding any official-looking notices. 'Route Barrée', or 'Road Closed' signs are regularly discounted by the French as being totally fanciful and they are often dismayed when they find the road actually is blocked.

There was a ford ahead and I drove into the water presuming I would emerge onto a dry road and arrive shortly. But the rivers were in flood and when I leaned out the window I could see the water was almost up to the door on my van and hear it burbling around the exhaust pipe at the back. If only I had heeded the sign! I was driving across fields covered with deep water and it was only the avenue of willow trees ahead that showed me where the submerged roadway was supposed to be. If the area was swamped like this surely the market would be cancelled? I had passed no other *brocanteurs'* vans. I was risking being trapped in a torrent. And I couldn't turn round and go back – there was a danger of slipping into one of the deep ditches.

The water was beginning to seep in round the bottom of the van door. Any second now the engine would cut out and I'd be stranded, forced to wade up to my waist through the icy waters, leaving all my stuff unprotected and at risk of being swept away.

The engine missed a beat and I was sure it was about to cut out when the incline began to rise, the waters dropped away, and I was driving on dry road again. I reached the outskirts of town with adrenalin coursing through my veins but thankful to have emerged unscathed.

I followed the signs to the centre and arrived in a large square, a covered plaza with stone arches surrounded by a rectangle of quaint old shops and buildings facing inwards. There were vans parked with *brocanteurs* setting up their trestle tables and opening parasols. Serge was among them and when he saw me he came over with a big grin on his face.

'Eh, Johnny, you didn't come in that way, did you?' He stepped back, looking at the water running off my van.

'Hope you packed your water wings. No one uses that road anymore. The river has changed its course; it's always flooded. You should have taken the other route with the bridges.' He waved towards the far side of the square. 'You're lucky you weren't drowned.' He shook his head in disbelief. 'Never mind, you made it, that's the main thing. Come on, I've spoken to the organisers and you can stall out next to me.' I followed him to a spot under the medieval stone arches.

'There we are, right next to the cafe and within strolling distance of the *boulangerie*. Never say I don't look after you.'

As I set up my table and umbrellas I looked around and noticed there were quite a few traders I knew. I was delighted to discover the *brocanteur* on my immediate left was my old pal Louis, the jazz-loving books and records dealer from Dax market. He was setting up his reconditioned antique gramophone, but when he saw me he came over and shook me warmly by the hand.

'Listen, John, this will interest you, I've got a whole pile of rare Charlie Parker and Bud Powell 78s I bought off an old jazzer in Biarritz at a knock-down price. You wait till you hear them.'

He showed me a pile of 'Vogue' records with their distinctive red and white labels. I flicked through and noted he had some of the original Gerry Mulligan, Chet Baker Quintet stuff from the fifties that included 'Walkin' Shoes', one of my all-time favourites.

'We'll be all right for a spot of bebop this afternoon then?' I said.

'You bet, John. Go, baby, go!' He began to tap out an irregular beat on the top of his trestle table.

I left him to it and continued unloading. I was lifting a heavy piece of nineteenth-century garden statuary of the god Pan playing a flute when someone grabbed me from behind and I turned to look up into the smiling face of Thibeau, one of the antique furniture dealers. He was built like one of his armoires and was a much-valued scrum forward playing regularly for his local rugby team.

'Eh, John, your luck's in. It's not every day you get those two for neighbours.' He nodded towards a stall opposite where a young woman in jeans and sweatshirt was bent over trestle tables covered with shiny pink satin cloths.

A balding man in camouflage combat trousers, with what was left of his hair tied back in a ponytail, was lolling back in a canvas chair with the legend DIRECTOR stencilled on the back. He watched nonchalantly as the woman unloaded painted furniture, cupboards, tables and chairs, all on her own from the back of a van. He didn't lift a finger to help her. She took out what looked to me like heavy boxes and staggered across with them to unpack on the trestle tables. They contained female undergarments which she picked out daintily piece by piece, arranging them tastefully on the pink cloths. The man yawned and stretched, and looked bored as the woman erected a series of rails and arranged a variety of sexy corsets and coloured basques for display.

'What a coquette!' said Thibeau, squeezing my arm. '*Mais la coquetterie est le fond de l'humeur des femmes, n'est-ce-pas?*' (But all women are basically coquettes, aren't they?)

He was over-excited, eyes popping, watching every move the woman made. I couldn't understand why he was so thrilled. She was attractive, but his reaction was over the top.

'*Putain!* It ought to be against the law,' he spluttered. 'It's more than flesh and blood can stand!'

'If it means so much, you can have my place,' I said.

'No, you enjoy it, John. You've not seen anything yet, believe me.'

I decided it must have been the sight of a young woman arranging sexy underwear that he found so erotic. I began to regard him in a new light. I hadn't got him pegged as a voyeur before, but now I wasn't so sure.

The man in combat trousers nodded at me and wished me '*Bonjour, voisin*' (Good day, neighbour). When I went over to shake hands he told me he was Bernard and that was his wife Angelique 'over there'.

Thibeau's face was a picture when she joined us and distributed kisses. They were warm and highly perfumed, so maybe that was what he liked about her.

When Bernard realised I was English, he livened up and got quite chatty. He insisted on religiously showing me his stock, which Angelique had just painstakingly arranged.

'You know the corset is making a big comeback in this country, John,' he said, matily. 'After fifty-odd years in the wilderness French women are starting to realise just how comfortable and alluring one can be.'

He unhooked a turquoise satin number trimmed with black lace and ran his fingers over it.

'This one dates from the beginning of the nineteenth century and would first have been worn in the bordellos by women of the night. It soon became popular with respectable women though. They didn't want to leave the art of seduction in the hands of just the professionals.' He beamed as he replaced it.

'But the corset wasn't always so risqué. A simple cotton whalebone corset to control the figure was considered a mark of respectability.' He passed me a long, beige cotton corset with brocade round the bust and suspenders decorated with gold fleur-de-lys.

'This is what they called *La Sylphide*, from the beginning of the nineteenth century. As you can see it wasn't so rigid and was quite comfortable to wear. Some of the tighter whalebone corsets had the effect of reducing a woman's dress size by about five or six sizes,' he said. 'Incredible, eh, John?'

I looked around to see if anyone was looking at me with a frilly corset in my hands. I was beginning to feel embarrassed and slightly pervy handling women's underwear in public, however historically interesting it was. Also, unlike Thibeau and Bernard, I wasn't finding floppy old corsets that much of a turn on. I excused myself, telling him I really ought to get back to setting up.

'Yes, I'll show you more about women's undergarments through the ages straight after lunch when it's a bit quieter,' he threatened. 'Some of these items are quite reasonably priced. You might want to pick out something as a present for your wife... or mistress.' He raised his eyebrows and made a suggestive clicking noise with his mouth.

'I'll look forward to that,' I lied.

I noticed Angelique had laid out a dust sheet, unloaded a stripped-down dressing table and was in the process of repainting it in the currently popular 'shabby chic' style. Serge had reappeared and was standing by watching, offering her little tips and pointing out bits she'd missed.

I went back to unloading stock and arranging it on my tables.

The sun was creeping over the medieval buildings on the square, warming the air and brightening up the early morning shadows. I munched away on a couple of croissants I'd bought from the nearby *boulangerie* and sipped at a large cup of creamy coffee, a takeaway from the cafe. These antiques fairs in small country towns could be a real pleasure. The residents were normally friendly and interested to see what little treasures they could unearth. Given the fact that they were comparatively isolated with only small local shops serving a widespread rural community, we *brocanteurs* were viewed as an alluring diversion: an exotic taste of the world outside. It is a tradition that has deep historical roots in France and despite the advent of the motor car, TV and Internet the *brocante* markets still retain a hint of their early glamour.

First to do the rounds were the dealers from the surrounding district, those with antiques shops in the far-flung towns and villages with an eye out for a bargain they could resell to the locals and tourists for a good profit. The accepted style of bartering was to haggle over the marked price, which was normally set high enough to allow a satisfactory reduction. I sold a flowery tea set to a woman who enthused about how she loved English porcelain, and an antique stick to an old gentleman.

Bernard next door appeared to be doing less well. He cast his eyes over my stuff and sighed.

'I've had a lot of prospective customers looking at my lingerie, John, and some interest in our painted furniture, but no one wants to part with their money. It's the peasants, they're a bit tight.'

Despite this, he still had a constant stream of other *brocanteurs* wanting to pass the time of day with him. I'd noticed several young men coming up to shake his hand and receive the obligatory warm-scented kiss from Angelique. They lurked about, hanging on her every word, and the older ones kept sneaking her little touches to emphasise a point they were making. She seemed to blossom from the attention, giggling and touching back.

My reverie was interrupted by a string of wild monkey whoops echoing across the square. These were followed by loud cat calls and screams of laughter. They sounded familiar. I asked Louis to keep an eye on my stall while I took a stroll around to investigate.

The source of all the noise turned out to be Serge sitting with Thibeau on a battered settee eating plates of oysters off a rusty old garden table. It was eight-thirty in the morning and they were gulping back oysters, swigging from straw-covered bottles of Chianti and yelling exuberantly.

'Eh, Johnny!' Serge leaped up. 'Come on, join us for breakfast.'

It was more of an order than an invitation. He picked up a grubby cup off the plastic sheet on the floor where Thibeau had some of his stuff displayed, slopped in some Chianti and handed it to me.

'Good health and plenty of money!'

He chinked my cup with his and quaffed it back. 'Help yourself to oysters, they give you…' he bent up a stiff forearm and waggled it suggestively about. I took this to mean they had aphrodisiac properties.

Thibeau picked up an oyster, slit open the shell with a knife and gave it to me. 'Go on, get that down your throat, John.' He chopped up a long loaf with several strokes of a rusty hand axe, offered me a thick wedge and watched as I lifted the shell to my mouth and touched the slippery stuff to my lips.

But it was no good, there was no way I could eat an oyster this early in the morning. I felt the bile rise in my throat.

'I'm sorry, it's a bit early for me,' I said, replacing the shell on the pile. 'Besides, I've already had my breakfast.'

'That's all right,' said Thibeau. 'We know you British don't care for food much.' He took the shell, threw back his head and gulped down the oyster flesh in one go. 'Or sex!' He made a loud smacking noise with his mouth, rubbed his stomach and belched enthusiastically.

Hang on a minute. I could go along with the lack of interest in food but not sex!

A pair of cheerful inebriates in the cafe opposite watched with bemused grins on their faces, then returned to the serious business of downing their first Ricards of the day.

'I'd better get to work,' I said, 'serve the customers.'

I made my way back to my stand. The morning bargain hunters were doing the rounds. I sold a little nineteenth-century barbotine Majolica jug in the shape a monkey playing a guitar, which I believed was probably either Italian or Portuguese, to a middle-aged man who went off happy, apparently well satisfied with his purchase. Helen had bought it in a *vide grenier*, or car boot sale, in our village. The man had asked if I would accept a cheque and when I told him no trouble as long as it was a French bank account he paid the amount in full without disputing the price. When this happens I tend to think the customer is more knowledgeable than I am and the item was probably worth a lot more. This can play on your mind so it's best to put it behind you, move on and concentrate on the next sale or you'll send yourself nuts. I was attempting to put my misgivings behind me when I glanced at the cheque and realised with horror he had omitted to sign it. I leaped up in a panic and rushed after him. But he had disappeared and I couldn't really remember what he looked like. I passed Serge, frantically scanning the crowds of people, waving the cheque in the air.

'What's up, Johnny?'

'God, that customer has forgotten to sign his cheque and now he's disappeared!'

'Here, let's see.' I gave it to him. 'I'll sort this out for you, Johnny.' Before I could stop him he produced a Bic, signed the cheque with a flourish and handed it back to me.

'You can't do that!' I cried, appalled.

'It happens all the time.' He gave a Gallic shrug. 'We always sign cheques when the customer forgets.'

I walked off, not feeling very comforted. When I looked at the cheque and saw the signature I did a double take. I ran back to Serge and shouted at him: 'You've signed this cheque Mickey Mouse! Mickey Mouse? You can't sign a cheque Mickey Mouse!'

'Don't worry, I always do that when someone forgets. My bank has never queried it.'

I stumbled back to my stand dumbfounded, with the cheque fluttering in my hand. Serge made the rules up as he went along. What was I thinking of? I pocketed the cheque and imagined what Helen would say when she saw it. I decided not to tell her and secretly sneak it into the bank.

The sun was almost overhead now and I was beginning to be glad of the shade afforded by my parasol. I was carefully wrapping up a particularly fine set of Limoges dinner plates with hand-painted designs of freshwater fishes for a charming elderly retired couple when a deafening braying sound blasted out in such close proximity and ear-splitting volume that I nearly dropped the lot. I slapped my hands to my ears to shut out the din and looked round to see Louis doing the same. It took a few teeth-rattling moments to grasp that this was the town air raid siren and a glance at my watch confirmed it was signalling *midi*, the holy French lunch hour. Many of these country towns continue to use their sirens in this way. Presumably when the war finished the mayor and townsfolk couldn't bear to dismantle such an authoritative and efficient instrument of aural torture, unlike the British who, having suffered years of the Blitz, couldn't wait to dump theirs along with all the other unpleasant memories.

Thibeau was quite right about one thing, though: compared to the French us British don't care about food. At least this used to be more true than maybe it is now.

When Helen and I first came to France and our knowledge of the language was fairly rudimentary we always wondered exactly what the French were talking so animatedly about. Was it philosophy or politics or the great questions of the day? As our vocabulary and translating skills improved we realised they were mainly discussing one thing: food.

The French can talk endlessly about what they ate or what they intend to eat, or the best way to prepare something they are going to eat. We used to think, God save us! How long are they going to go on and on about food? Isn't there something more interesting to talk about? What on earth's the matter with them? But now we've been living in France for so long, wouldn't you know it, we're just the same. We talk about food, too. We're as tiresome about it as they are. Also, we're spoilt as far as food is concerned. We are disappointed if the food we are served up when we eat out is not good and appetising. We are picky and feel let down when we get something bland or tasteless as if the cook hasn't bothered to even try.

With the aftershock of the air raid siren still ringing in our ears Louis and I covered up our stuff and headed for the restaurant opposite, fought through the other *brocanteurs* and ordered an aperitif for Louis and an orange juice for me. Sitting at the bar I recognised Jesus Raines, the guitarist who lost his family when his caravan caught fire.

'Eh, Johnny, how you going, *en forme*?' He seemed more cheerful than when we first met at St Michelle and appeared pleased to see me.

'You know what today is, Johnny? The twenty-first of June. And you know what that means, don't you?'

Of course, La Fête de la Musique! I'd quite forgotten all about it. Every year throughout France on this date every French musician worth his salt gets to play somewhere for the evening. All the music bars, clubs and most of the cafes feature groups or solo musicians, the only drawback being that ever since I'd been in France it had pissed down with rain on the night of the *fête*. I don't know why this should be, but as a lot of the gigs take place in the open air the weather always proved to be something of a dampener to the proceedings.

'There's going to be a big jam session tonight. You ought to come along,' said Jesus.

'Maybe I will,' I said.

'Hey, you've got to meet my son Buddy, the one I told you about.' He signalled across to a hip young guy with a shaved head and a short trimmed beard who came across. Jesus put his arm round his shoulder. 'He's dragged himself away from all his charming Parisian women to come down and visit his poor old dad.'

Buddy smiled tolerantly. 'Dad told me all about you,' he said, shaking my hand. 'Fancy a blow tonight?'

Did I ever! I didn't get much chance with most of the markets taking place at the weekends.

'And where are you sleeping tonight?' asked Jesus.

'In the van,' I said, 'as usual.'

'I won't hear of it. You must stay with me. I have a comfortable spare bed in my caravan.'

What could I say? To turn down the offer would have been rude. Besides, I wasn't relishing a night humped up in the van.

'Meet us here when the fair finishes and we'll go for a meal.'

I promised I would and joined Louis and Serge at a table. As I ate my lunch I thought about Jesus' invitation to stay in his caravan. He was still sitting at the bar with his son. He turned, saw me, took a deep drag on a cigarette and waved his glass at me in a toast.

I felt a small stab of anxiety. There was no way he could set fire to his caravan a second time, surely?

14

JIVE MUSIC AND OWLS

The afternoon was hot and sticky. Louis had gone off excited with a little old man who said he had a pile of jazz albums at home he wanted to sell off cheaply. As I sat drowsily in my canvas chair recovering from lunch, my eyes kept straying across to Bernard's van.

I was intrigued. Angelique had just climbed in the back and pulled the doors to. Then Serge appeared, gave me a wave and went in after her. I couldn't imagine what was going on. There was no sign of Bernard.

A few minutes later, to my astonishment, Angelique re-emerged completely transformed. Gone were the jeans and sweatshirt. She was now wearing a classy designer frock with sexy patterned black stockings and white high heels. Serge was behind her helping her do the buttons up the back. He gave me another little wave, looked slightly embarrassed, and left.

Angelique looked fantastic. She shimmied over to her stand and began rearranging the lingerie. I was changing my mind about her. Thibeau was right. Watching her move the lacy knickers and bras around dressed like this was proving to be quite a turn on.

She was trying to sell a red satin corset with a black lacy trim to a young mum, who was tempted, but she had a child in a pushchair and a toddler and I think maybe it was too expensive for her. Angelique was giving her the works – a steady stream of sales patter pointing out the merits of the garment, stroking it, caressing it, turning it this way and that. Sunbeams flashed on the shiny satin. She tilted her head, opened her beautiful eyes wide and made little moues with her red-lipsticked mouth.

The woman had decided she'd have to think about it and maybe bring her husband along to show him, when Angelique did something that took my breath away. She reached behind her neck, undid a couple of hooks, and in one swift movement pulled her dress up and over her head. Her underwear was light and filmy, and her body glowed unbearably white in the brilliant sunlight. She stepped daintily into the corset, positioned it until it was comfortable and asked the woman to help her lace it up tight. I held my breath as the woman tugged at the red laces, tying bows as instructed.

The result was truly stunning. The corset pinched in Angelique's waist and lifted her breasts. She looked like a dream film star from the fifties. Bernard was right; these undergarments worked wonders.

I turned away, unable to gaze any longer on a vision of such loveliness, and was confronted by the tableau of Serge and

Thibeau standing behind me grinning like a pair of Notre Dame gargoyles.

'See, what did I tell you?' said Thibeau, punching me on the arm. 'Was I right or what?'

Serge was smiling sweetly with a look of indulgence on his face. I got the impression he might have a crush on her. But dream on – she was completely out of his league.

Looking at Angelique standing semi-naked in the red satin corset reminded me of Helen in our group True Life Confessions when she used to go on stage in skimpy outfits not dissimilar to this one. I could buy it for her! If I was especially nice she might consent to wear it round the house for old times' sake and give me a thrill.

Bernard came weaving across the square from a nearby restaurant. He looked sated, like he'd partaken of a decent lunch while Angelique was hard at it.

'Eh, Bernard! Angelique is looking as lovely as ever,' shouted Thibeau.

Bernard hardly gave her a second glance, plonked himself down in his director's chair and lounged back with his hands behind his head.

Despite the astonishing demonstration, the young mum was still unable to make up her mind and hurried off, promising to return with her husband. I was convinced if he had been there the sight of Angelique's semi-clad form would have had him reaching zombie-like for his wallet.

'You see this basque that Angelique is wearing, John?' said Bernard, slurring his words.

I nodded and gulped.

'It is called *la guêpière*, or as you say in English, 'the Waspy', invented by Marcel Rochas here in France. This is similar to the one worn by Martine Carol in Christian-Jaque's movie *Adorables Créatures*.'

'Really?' To be honest I didn't give a damn. I was fast losing interest in Bernard's historical facts.

'Very sexy, no?'

'Er, yes.' I didn't want to admit that I'd been lusting after his wife.

He pulled himself upright and tottered over.

'Here, give me a hand please, John.' He began to pull at the laces. 'Help me undo these bows, would you?'

I fumbled at the laces, trying not to look at Angelique's white flesh.

'I hope to God that trade picks up this afternoon,' he said. 'People don't seem to want to pay the proper price for nice lingerie anymore. I can't understand it. We've not sold a thing.

I caught Angelique's eye and blushed. She giggled. 'You're not shy, are you, John? That is so English. How sweet.'

I fumbled at the knots, feeling like a lurker, sensing the heat from her body and guiltily breathing in the aroma of her exotic perfume.

Later that evening, I loaded up the van and strolled over to the cafe to grab a bite to eat before the music started. It had been a good day on the market and I was pleased and relaxed, although I was still vaguely uneasy about Serge's Mickey Mouse signature on that cheque. I saw Buddy at a corner table. He gave me a wave, inviting me over. He looked over to where his dad was lolling across the bar.

'He's pickled as usual, I'm afraid, John. I worry about him when I'm not here to look after him. It's not just his drinking.

He gambles and he's got unpaid debts. His life is a mess. He can't forgive himself for what happened and because he can't play any more all his emotions are bottled up inside like some kind of terrible unexploded bomb. It breaks my heart to see him like this.'

We helped his dad up and out across the square where the last few traders were finishing packing up. We made our way down a series of little streets and alleys to a cafe bar called 'Le Gainsbourg', with an illuminated hanging sign bearing a cartoon illustration of the much-revered, scruffy-but-talented French singer and composer.

Inside a band of musicians were setting up their gear on a small corner stage. While they ran through a couple of numbers from their set I went over to Jesus, who appeared to have pulled himself together. He was sitting drinking coffee. The walk in the fresh air had sobered him up.

'Well then, John, what do you think of my son Buddy?' It was amazing. He was almost his old self.

'He's a great musician,' I said. 'And *très sympa*. You've every reason to be proud.'

He smiled, pleased. 'And he can play, can't he? It's in his blood. You know, John, my family is related to Django, the great guitarist who took the musical traditions of our people the Manouche and mixed them with jazz and blues to create the Gypsy jazz style. My father was also a great guitarist and a close friend of Django's in Paris in the thirties. He taught me to play when I was just a kid.' He held up his crooked hand and stared surprised, as if seeing it for the first time. 'If it wasn't for this, John...' He looked away.

I knew exactly what he meant to say. If it wasn't for his burnt hand he could join in and play alongside his son on stage. And that was what he'd like to do more than anything else in the world. I really liked the guy. I felt as if I'd known him all my life.

When he turned back there wasn't a trace of self-pity in his expression. 'You know, Django taught himself to play again even though he lost the use of the third and fourth fingers of his left hand in a fire. But my hand is completely useless. There's not much I can do about it. Ironical when you think about it.'

The owner of the bar invited us out the back into his private dining room where his wife had laid on a meal for the musicians in the band. Buddy assured me this level of hospitality was quite normal. I told him that musicians in England were lucky if they managed to eat their home-made sandwiches in the toilet before a gig. He laughed. He thought I was making it up.

I was enjoying hanging out with a bunch of musicians again. I was offered a beer and accepted, thinking I could handle just the one. Then, as the wine came round during the meal I knocked back one glass, then another. I was in my element, laughing and joking, having a great time. My defences were down.

The rest of the evening began to merge into an alcoholic blur. I remember sitting in on drums and then singing a couple of blues numbers and playing a bit of harmonica. I can vaguely recall Serge and Angelique and Thibeau being in the audience, congratulating me and insisting on buying me more drinks at the bar. I vaguely recall watching Serge and Angelique jiving together and everyone cheering them on. And there's a flash of me and Jesus arm in arm dancing and shouting along with the rest of the audience to a spirited version of 'I've Got My Mojo Working'. But after that it's all a blank.

I woke up in total darkness with no idea where I was. My mouth felt like it was full of sand. I reached out, groping around for clues. I tried to sit up and bumped my head.

I believe it was an Edgar Allan Poe story I'd read as a boy (I'm not one hundred per cent sure of the author) about the man with an unreasoned fear of being buried alive who wakes up in total darkness and feels the lid of his closed coffin. Anyway, this had obviously made a big impression on me because the horror of it flashed through my mind.

I WAS BURIED ALIVE!

I was sealed up in my coffin. But I wasn't dead!

I reached out with one arm and felt... the side of the coffin!

Then I panicked.

I screamed and hit out with both arms, rolled sideways and fell, landing hard. I lay on my back gasping for breath and heard a groan. The light came on, blinding me.

As my eyes adjusted I could see I was in a caravan and had just fallen out of bed. Jesus was lying on another bunk bed across the way. He peered at me, surprised, then turned over and went back to sleep.

When I stood up I was wearing just underpants and a wine-stained T-shirt.

I staggered about looking for something cool to quench my thirst. I searched the little shelves around a stove built into a corner of the caravan. On these shelves decoratively juxtapositioned were little china ornaments. Nothing to drink here, but the little ornaments... they looked familiar.

Closer inspection revealed they were all little owls of various sizes and species.

In a flash I remembered my AA minder, the one Alcoholics Anonymous had given me when I was trying to give up drinking. My heart sank. I was having an 'owl moment'! After all the years of relative sobriety here I was back at square one again... a confirmed alcoholic with a king-size hangover.

15

HAUNTINGS, HOMESICKNESS AND HOLY WATER

It was Serge's idea to do a fair near Lourdes. 'There's all those rich hoteliers and shopkeepers there; they earn a fortune from the faithful. All that money and nothing to spend it on but holy water. They'll fall over themselves to buy our stuff.'

Oh yeah, right, I thought. But I quite liked the idea. Lourdes is a three-hour drive from us in the foothills of the Pyrenees. It was the end of August and the last weekend of the holiday period so we could possibly do well.

'I'm up for it if we can go a day earlier and visit Lourdes itself,' I said. I remembered someone telling me that if you liked kitsch religious paraphernalia then Lourdes was *the* place to go.

'Of course we can,' said Serge. 'I had exactly the same idea myself. You know St Bernadette was a poor Basque, just like me, Johnny.'

I didn't want to appear ignorant but admitted I knew nothing about St Bernadette.

'You're no Catholic, are you?' said Serge.

'I was brought up a Methodist,' I said, 'but you could say I'm lapsed.'

He stared back at me blankly. He had no idea what I was talking about. But since my last drunken episode I was determined not to fall off the wagon again. I hadn't told Helen about it. I only hoped I wasn't going to have to turn to religion to keep me sober. After all, when I'd banked Serge's Mickey Mouse cheque without telling her it had passed with no comeback whatsoever.

'Helen would like to come along,' I said. 'We've talked about visiting Lourdes and never got round to it. She'd be disappointed if she missed out.'

'Of course, Johnny.' His eyes twinkled. 'You know how much I like your wife. She's so charming. It'll be a real pleasure to see her.'

He was acting like Pepé Le Pew again. The first time he met Helen he'd surprised me by telling me how attractive she was, and how lucky I was to have found such a desirable woman. I'd been flattered but taken aback. Helen, for her part, had been underwhelmed by him. She'd found him slightly amusing but didn't really like him. I might have a bit of difficulty persuading her to come along. But she needed a break and if truth be known I was worried about her. Recently she'd taken to watching daytime TV, avidly following the antiques and car boot programmes.

'What else am I supposed to do?' she argued. 'The people who buy in auction to sell in the *vide greniers* have pushed prices up so high it's hardly worth bothering to go any more.

And the market in England is flooded with French antiques so we can't sell there. It's all going down the drain and I'm trying to mug up on English antiques in case we have to move back.

Her inactivity, I knew, was caused by more than the state of the antiques market. The death of our Staffordshire bull terrier Spike had knocked us both for six. I'd even hung his old collar on our bedpost and polishing it up and touching it gave me some sort of comfort. But Helen had found it difficult to get his death in perspective and she was unable to grieve properly. Her mum had died two years earlier and she was still coming to terms with that. She was bereft and her unhappiness had manifested itself as an overpowering feeling of homesickness.

'I've not got anything to go back to England for since Mum died,' she had said, 'but I still feel homesick. It's awful.'

I was at a loss and unable to comfort her properly. The thought of going back to England to live wasn't really an option for me. I enjoyed the return trips we made but I was settled in France and loved my life here. I couldn't imagine packing it all in and returning home.

'I heard the whispering voices again today,' she said.

Oh no, not the whispering voices again!

Maybe I should explain about the whispering voices, in case you think Helen might have gone completely over the edge.

The 300-year-old peasant cottage we live in appears to be haunted. Not all the time, but off and on. The old boy who had owned it lived in the house all his life, as did his parents before him. When his mother died he lived there alone, growing all his own produce and making his own wine (there is a small vineyard running to the edge of our land). The isolated house we took over was just as he'd left it when he died: small rooms with religious pictures and mementoes; beds carefully made; shaving kit laid out on the stone *évier* (sink) ready for the following morning. His name was Gaston. I had a habit of thanking him out loud when I was doing something in the *atelier* (workshop).

Time and again when I needed a special drill bit or certain sized screw it would suddenly be there, waiting for me to find it. Saying 'Thank you, Gaston' seemed like the right thing to do, and I had this strange feeling I was acknowledged.

Sometimes we would hear the distinctive sound of an old Citroën 2CV pulling up at the end of the drive and rush out to find the yard deserted, just the cooing of Gaston's pigeons and a faint whiff of a Gitanes cigarette. This happened so often we took to ignoring it.

As we set about renovating the house we noticed that most of the inner doors had small crucifixes made out of what appeared to be dried-up pastry stuck to them. I rationalised that this must have been some common religious custom but I've never seen anything like them before or since.

Tony, a carpenter friend from England, who was staying with us while building a staircase in the barn adjoining the house, came rushing through one evening looking shaken. He had been working in the *grenier* (loft) when he looked down and saw the figure of an old man standing in the barn. Tony thought it was probably a neighbour come to see what we were up to, but when he went to investigate the figure had disappeared.

Then there were the whispering voices. From the moment we moved in Helen swore she could hear faint voices, as if people were still living in the house but just slightly removed from our perception. Sometimes I imagined I could hear them too. But despite this the atmosphere in the house felt generally welcoming. That was until we decided to knock down one of the interior wattle and daub walls.

The room we decided was to be our bedroom had a small medieval-type window, and at the far end a small enclosed separate room with a bed in it. We think this windowless cell had been Gaston's mother's bedroom and she probably died there. It wasn't much use to us and I set about dismantling the walls with a sledgehammer. The dried mud and straw created a haze of dust as it collapsed and I was shovelling the mess into a wheelbarrow when I came across a small faded cloth bag tied up with a piece of animal hide. I opened it and found what appeared to be pieces of human hair and chicken feathers rolled into a ball and smeared with something that had long since dried into a dark, dusty mess. I showed it to Helen and she shivered and suggested I make a hole in the wall and seal it back in. I did this, swept up and we went out for a pizza.

When we returned later in the evening we got a shock. Everything had changed. Whereas the atmosphere in the house had been warm and welcoming it was now cold and malevolent, so much so that we couldn't face sleeping there and decamped to our caravan behind the barn.

We woke up the next morning thinking we had imagined it, but when we re-entered the house it was almost as if someone were screaming silently at us, warning us to leave. It was such a strong feeling that we didn't question it. This was serious. We had to do something.

I surmised, in desperation, that whoever or whatever lived in the house had assumed I was trying to knock the place down. It sounds crazy now, but I went into the bedroom and walked about talking in French, explaining that we weren't going to harm anything, but just needed more room. We had no intention of destroying the house. On the contrary, we intended to keep all its original features and reinstate it to its former glory.

This had no discernable effect. The house maintained its malevolent atmosphere. But we eventually managed to overcome our fear and move back in.

Not long after this I woke up in the middle of the night as if someone had touched me on the shoulder. I opened my eyes and saw a white kitten creeping across the big oak beam in our bedroom. When it reached the wall it walked along the top of the door and then climbed down the side, stopping for a moment, backlit from the light in the hall. It shone with an eerie luminescence, and it was only when it had climbed back up the way it had come and disappeared that I realised that this was impossible; the room was in pitch darkness. There were heavy shutters on the windows and no light in the hall. The animal had been glowing with an inner light of its own. I must have cried out loud because I felt Helen grip my arm.

'Did you see that?' she gasped.

We were taken aback when her description of what she had seen matched mine exactly. But at least a ghostly kitten wasn't something to worry about. It wasn't malevolent or threatening. Over the next few weeks the house gradually returned to normal. Even the whispering voices receded. Helen said they were so faint she hardly noticed them any more.

But now they were back.

I didn't like the sound of this. We definitely needed a break away. I decided to put Serge's suggestion about a trip to Lourdes to her.

'There's that fair near Lourdes this weekend,' I said. 'Serge and I were thinking of going to Lourdes the day before. Why don't you come with us? We could take the caravan and have a little holiday.'

'All right,' she said.

It was easier than I thought.

That weekend the three of us were sitting outside a cafe on the main street of Lourdes enjoying the sunshine. The air was fresh and clean, as if it had just blown in from across the snow-covered mountain peaks of the Pyrenees – which it probably had.

Helen had perked up slightly, mostly due to the fact that she was fussing Robespierre. Serge had brought him along 'to get used to people'.

Serge was shamelessly flirting with Helen, turning on his Gallic charm.

'You should bring your beautiful wife along more often, Johnny.' He squeezed her hand. 'This is fun, isn't it?'

Helen withdrew her hand and carried on stroking Robespierre. I couldn't help recalling how Serge had boasted to me about what he'd got up to when he was in the army with the wives of English tourists. How he'd got the husbands paralytic drunk and lured the wives away and 'made love to them' in the public toilets. I wasn't impressed but I'd better make sure I stayed on the wagon just in case.

Serge flicked his fingers to catch the waiter's eye and ordered himself another Ricard. 'Are you sure you won't have a beer or anything, Johnny?'

There you are, he was up to his old tricks again.

'No thanks,' I said, guiltily remembering my lapse at La Fête de la Musique.

'Just a coffee, is it?' He pronounced 'coff-ee' in the English manner. It was his little joke.

'My cousin came and saw the Pope when he came to Lourdes,' he said. 'Young girls screaming and fainting. It was like being at a pop concert.' He knocked back his Ricard and suggested we take a stroll round the gift shops. The high street was crammed with them.

Helen and I were astonished at the bad taste of some of the souvenirs.

There were St Bernadette holy cushions, St Bernadette sacred slippers, St Bernadette consecrated potties, even St Bernadette blessed backscratchers. I toyed with the idea of a St Bernadette miraculous plastic water-filled dome. When you shook it bits of glitter swirled around a garish grotto with St Bernadette kneeling at the Virgin's feet. But in the end I couldn't bring myself to buy it. Despite my supposed interest in kitsch religious memorabilia Helen and I were beginning to feel faintly queasy at the sheer grossness of some of the products on sale here.

'Seeing all these shops cashing in, I can't help thinking about Jesus driving the money lenders and merchants out of the temple,' said Helen.

'I can imagine him having a similar reaction to this lot,' I said.

Serge was unfazed and insisted we buy blue plastic water flasks with carrying straps and screw lids decorated with religious depictions of the Lourdes miracle. 'We need them for collecting our holy water from the grotto.'

I was leafing through a booklet on the counter in an attempt to try and find out more about St Bernadette and the real story of Lourdes when the shopkeeper – a formidable grey-haired woman in a twinset – snatched it from my hands.

'If you're not going to buy that then don't read it.' She replaced it on the counter and walked off.

Serge thought this was a great laugh.

'Don't mess with these shopkeepers, Johnny. They're like straight-laced school mistresses, they don't take any shit.'

'I was only trying to find out a bit more about St Bernadette.'

'Let's go and have lunch,' he said. 'I can tell you everything you need to know.'

We found a restaurant with a good set meal and as we ate Serge told us the Lourdes story with an attention to detail that surprised me.

'St Bernadette is the People's Saint,' he said, 'in much the same way as your Diana was the People's Princess. When she was only fourteen she had a vision of a beautiful girl in the mouth of a grotto here while she was out gathering firewood. The girl in the vision was small – the same size as Bernadette herself – and said she wanted to be her friend.

'After that Bernadette kept coming back and seeing the vision so regularly that all the people in the village, as Lourdes was then, took to following her out and watching. They couldn't see the vision themselves but they were so impressed that word soon spread and crowds came from far and wide to watch her kneeling in prayer, gazing up at the grotto. The beautiful girl told Bernadette to dig in the rock with her fingers and drink the muddy water that appeared.

But when Bernadette turned round with her face all muddy and covered in bits of grass the people watching cried out with revulsion and wondered why they'd come at all. "This cave used to be a pigsty," they said, "and now she's become just like a pig."

'Well, that blew Bernadette's reputation completely and the local police and priests had her in with her father and mother to try and persuade her to stop going up to the cave and causing such a fuss. But she carried on and the people forgot the muddy face incident and her fame spread, especially when a fresh water spring flowed from the rock where she'd dug a hole and the water was reputed to have miraculous healing powers.

'Needless to say, the Church jumped on the bandwagon and decided the vision was of the Virgin Mary. A famous sculptor was commissioned to create a statue like the beautiful girl in the vision. He worked away and when he'd finished it everyone said how wonderful it was and so like the Virgin it was uncanny.

'But when Bernadette saw it she cried out: "No, that's not her!" And the poor old sculptor was crushed and said it was the most disappointing moment of his life. But they put it up in the mouth of the grotto anyway and it's still there to this day. And since then they've built a basilica and churches and God-knows-what on the site and so many people have had miraculous cures the Pope decided to make Bernadette a saint.'

'Do you believe in it?' asked Helen. 'Do you believe in the miracle?'

'I believe Bernadette had a vision,' said Serge. 'But it could have been because she was hallucinating from starvation and sickness. She had cholera at the time. And people were so bored they needed something to spice up their lives a bit.'

'But I thought you were a good Catholic,' I said.

'I was – once. But like you I'm lapsed. I don't know what I believe any more.'

'So why did you come here?' said Helen.

'Well, it can't do any harm, can it? And I've not been to Lourdes since I was a kid. I thought it might do me some good.'

He unscrewed one of the plastic flasks and sniffed at it. 'You may not believe this but when I was a young lad I dreamed of becoming a priest.'

This was such an unexpected gem of information that I found it hard to keep a straight face. Helen was more sympathetic. I couldn't be sure but I had a feeling she was warming to him.

'But we seldom end up fulfilling our dreams do we?' he said. Let's go and fill our flasks with some of this famous holy water.'

We followed the signs out of the town centre up to an imposing gated entrance leading onto a grand drive which swept up to the various churches that had sprung up over the years. It was hard to imagine now what the place had been like in Bernadette's day.

There was a sign on the gates in several languages saying 'NO DOGS ALLOWED'.

I agreed to take Robespierre back to the van while Serge and Helen went up to the grotto. As I walked back through the town with Robespierre pulling on his lead I had a vision myself. It was of Serge trying to lure Helen up to the toilets.

I lifted Robespierre up onto the front seat of the van and wound down the windows halfway. The sun was strong now and I didn't want him to overheat. I poured some Evian water into a plastic dog bowl and positioned it where he could get to it if he was thirsty. He had his nose up on the glass, watching me forlornly as I walked off.

16

THE MIRACLE

Back at the entrance gates the crowds were streaming up the drive towards the Basilica. What had drawn them all here to Lourdes? Not everyone could be sick or crippled and in need of a miracle cure. There were a few tourists in shorts with cameras slung round their necks. But a large proportion of the visitors looked well-scrubbed and smartly dressed, as if on their way to attend Sunday mass.

A few little old ladies went past clutching prayer books. And then, surprisingly, a line of what looked like hospital trolleys being pushed by nurses. Each trolley supported a sick patient wrapped in blankets. They appeared to have emerged from a hospital building situated in the grounds. Were miracle cures a regular occurrence here at Lourdes? If not, it seemed cruel to offer such slim hope to desperately sick people.

I started to worry about Helen and Serge. They had promised to meet me here.

A group of leather-jacketed bikers, one wearing a neck brace and hobbling on crutches, went by, jostling each other. And then a party of handicapped children in wheelchairs pushed by nuns.

Still no sign of Helen and Serge.

I was about to give up and ask someone where the nearest toilets were when I spotted Helen's red hair bobbing through the throng and she emerged smiling and waving at me.

She hugged me and squeezed my hand and I felt ashamed of myself.

'Where's Serge?' I said.

'Filling our bottles with holy water. Come on!'

She was energised like I hadn't seen her for ages.

We found him by a line of chrome taps set in a wall – the push-button type you often find in gents' urinals. He was tightening the tops on our blue plastic flasks. When he saw us he unscrewed the removable beaker on one and squirted some water into it.

He handed it to me. 'Take a swig of that. See if it makes you a nicer person.'

I drank some down. It tasted like ordinary water to me.

'No, still the same miserable bastard,' I said, handing it back. I looked at Helen and pulled a face.

'Helen's already had some,' said Serge. 'She's gone all holy. Don't tell me you hadn't noticed.'

'I had actually,' I said, and they both laughed.

'We can go up and look at the Basilica,' said Serge. 'Then come back later in the evening for the candlelit service at the grotto.'

We strolled up towards the grandiose Basilica of the Immaculate Conception. It seemed overblown and hardly in keeping with the story of St Bernadette that Serge had told us. Maybe the original intention had been to magnify God in all his glory. But it appeared to me that the Church had hijacked something simple and moving to use for its own political ends. It reminded me of everything I found distasteful about organised religion.

Inside there was a vast painting on the ceiling, purportedly of the Virgin Mary.

'Oh my God! It looks almost like a devil to me,' said Helen.

'Yeah,' I said. 'It's like a big, floating, evil face.'

'I think it's really creepy,' said Helen.

'Looks like they had trouble with their painters as well as their sculptors,' said Serge.

'Where's the grotto?' said Helen. 'This place is horrid.'

'You know, you're right,' said Serge.

We followed him out into the fresh air and down some steps to a lower level. With his bright blue plastic flasks of holy water hanging round his neck he looked like a big kid let loose in Disneyland.

The grotto itself was the complete antithesis of the puffed up Basilica. It almost seemed to be cowering down beneath it, an unprepossessing, half-moon shaped cave of white rock inset with a coloured statue of the Virgin. There were lots of ancient crutches hanging pathetically from the stone walls, but strangely enough, no shiny new ones. Maybe something miraculous had happened here in the past but there was no concrete evidence of recent cures.

A handful of people drifted by, looking at the statue and up at the crutches. It felt like we were in a museum that had no real relevance to the world today.

'Is that it?' I asked Serge. 'Is that all the grotto is? I was expecting at least a decent-sized cave.'

'It's not what I expected either,' said Helen.

'It's a bit drab,' I said.

'Yes, and very sad,' she said, 'with all those crutches.'

'I reckon they just hung them there to impress the punters,' I said. 'Probably the same time they put up the statue. I'm not fooled.'

'Please don't make fun of it,' said Serge. 'I told you I wanted to be a priest once. I still have finer feelings you know, despite being a *brocanteur*.'

I couldn't help smiling, thinking of some of his more recent tricks.

'I don't think I could work up the enthusiasm to come to a candlelit service tonight.' I said. 'Maybe we should skip it.'

'Let's see how we feel later,' said Helen, 'after Serge has checked into a hotel.'

We left the grotto, climbed the stone steps and walked back up the drive to the main gates. There was still a constant flow of people drifting in and out.

As we drew nearer to our parked van we could see Robespierre's face up at the window.

'Do you think he's been looking out for us like that all the time?' said Helen.

'Of course he has,' said Serge. 'That's one faithful little dog – a real character.'

Most of the hotels were full, but Serge eventually found one with a spare room that accepted dogs. The proprietor – a diminutive rosy-cheeked woman with neat blonde hair – was yet another doll collector. She looked like a little doll herself. We could see into her living room. There were dolls everywhere; a line of them sitting on a couch and even more up on the mantelpiece. Some of them looked like antiques and Serge's eyes were popping as he leaned over to get a better view. I knew he was trying to spot any valuable ones.

When I took his arm and hissed 'No!' at him, he rubbed his eyes, crossed himself and smiled sheepishly, as if reminded of the sanctity of his pilgrimage here.

'Don't worry, Johnny, I'm not here for business – I'm here for my soul.'

He invited us to dine with him before we returned to our caravan, which was parked on a nearby site. But as we ate our dinner in the hotel's dining room, I noticed he couldn't stop his eyes straying to the various little alcoves and shelves where several dolls had been decoratively perched.

The evening was balmy and surprisingly warm with a thin crescent moon and a breathtaking sky bright with stars. After dinner we decided we would go to the candlelit service after all. With Robespierre sitting up front in the van we drove across town and parked within walking distance of the grotto.

Serge patted Robespierre on the head. 'Now look after the van while we're gone and bite anyone who tries to break in.'

'I'm training him up to guard my stuff,' he explained. 'He may be small now, but you wait till he gets his big-boy's teeth.'

We followed the flow of people through to the main gates and wandered around aimlessly until we found ourselves high up on the flat roof of the Basilica looking out over the steeples and minarets. The scene below had a magical quality. The lights from hundreds of candles and lanterns moved slowly in a shimmering river of tiny flames as the crowds swirled round the grotto.

Helen and I stood holding hands. Our eyes were drawn from the sparkling candles below to the vastness of the night sky above. The stars themselves were like billions of twinkling candles and we gazed up at the vastness of the firmament in wonder. We were just two small beings on the surface of a planet floating in a far-flung corner of the universe. What were we doing here? What was it all about?

I felt a thump against my shoulder. Someone had barged into me, bringing me back to earth with a bang. I swung round to see whoever had done it run off and disappear behind a section of stone roofing. At first I thought it must have been an accident. But then the individual reappeared and circled back through the crowd towards us.

The thought crossed my mind that it was someone who knew us having a joke. But as the character got closer I could see it was a young man in his early twenties with a wild expression and staring eyes.

He sidled along beside a parapet and as he passed close by hissed at me: 'Satan's spawn – you must be gone from this sacred place!'

The bloke had a strong German accent. I could hardly believe my ears. But for some reason it struck me as comical. Why had he picked on me? Did I look like Satan's spawn? Surely not.

Helen was amused at first, but then worried. 'He looks nasty. Maybe we should keep out of his way.'

Serge had seen what had happened. I tried to explain about the 'Satan's spawn' bit, but had difficulty translating this into French.

He got the gist of it though. 'There are all sorts of maniacs about these days, Johnny. Best be careful, eh?'

We watched out to see if the guy would reappear. When there was no sign of him I tried to regain some of the calm and tranquillity we'd been enjoying earlier. But the mood had gone.

We looked over the wall at the scene below. Several priests were leading a procession from the Basilica towards the grotto. They were joined by more people holding candles, following silently.

'I think the service is about to begin,' said Helen.

As we headed for the stairs I felt bony fingers bite into the flesh at the back of my arm and I turned to look into the eyes of the German weirdo who'd bothered me earlier. He pulled himself in close. I could feel his hot breath on my face.

'I haf been warning you already Beelzebub, you must be gone from this...'

And here his words were choked off. His eyes widened as he was jerked back almost off his feet. It was only then I realised that Serge had him by the collar and seat of his pants. He frogmarched him across the roof, dragged him up against a parapet and held him bent over against the brickwork. We watched amazed as Serge cuffed him lightly across the back of his head, hoisted him upright and began to berate him, poking his finger in his chest to emphasise what he was saying. The poor bloke looked shocked, pulling back in disbelief. And when Serge pinched his cheek and mockingly slapped him across the forehead with the palm of his hand he recoiled in horror and reeled back to stagger off towards the stairs.

Serge rejoined us, smiling to himself.

'What on earth did you say to him?' asked Helen.

'Nothing much. I just told him that Johnny was the Antichrist sent from hell to destroy the earth, and that I was his Black Angel. If he dared bother you again he would be killed and cast into outer darkness to rot for all eternity.'

'He might have had a bit of difficulty grasping all that,' I said. 'He was German. I doubt if he spoke much French.'

'He understood all right,' said Serge. 'He went off as if all the demons in hell were after him.'

'Thanks,' I said. 'I appreciate it.' There was a note of admiration in my voice.

He put his arm round my shoulder. 'Think nothing of it, Johnny. Eh! He was a junkie, high as a kite on God knows what. There's no telling what *pourri* like that will do.'

'Quite,' I said. And made a mental note to try not to offend Serge in future if I could possibly help it.

We descended the staircase to ground level and followed the flow until we were in the middle of the hushed crowd standing in front of the grotto. We could hear a low murmur from the priests conducting the service.

The money-grabbing gift shops, the puffed up Basilica and my experience on the roof with the mad German hadn't put me in a very receptive mood for tuning in to things of a deeper or spiritual nature. I was now totally convinced that Lourdes was an elaborate confidence trick designed to magnify the power of the Roman Catholic Church. I was of a completely disbelieving frame of mind, slightly revolted with myself for bothering to have come here in the first place.

But as I stood watching the people standing silently all around me, their faces lit by the glow of the lanterns, I suddenly felt an incredible force hit me square in the chest.

It took my breath away.

It was emanating from the rock face and the sheer strength of it was overwhelming.

Helen held me tightly round the waist. I looked at Serge. His eyes were all swimmy. The three of us were riveted to the spot.

It was as if some benevolent alien being had suddenly arrived, radiating all-powerful love and compassion.

I'm not sure how long we stood there entranced. Time seemed to stand still. But eventually the strength of the emanation diminished, the service finished and we drifted towards the entrance gate with everyone else still enthralled. All my cynicism had melted away.

It had been an incredible experience. One we would never forget.

Was this what the villagers felt watching Bernadette kneeling in front of the grotto? If so, I could see why the Church had wanted to muscle in on the act. But was it a holy manifestation or something else?

We reached the van and as I unlocked the door Robespierre jumped around on the seat, ecstatic to have us back. I'm not sure how it happened, but as I unlocked the door on the driver's side he bounced excitedly towards me, lost his footing and plummeted over the edge. I tried to catch him but he slipped through the gap and hit the pavement giving a little squeal of pain as he did so. He went to get up but pitifully fell on his face again as his front legs gave way.

Serge rushed round in a panic and swept him up.

'Is he all right? He's not hurt, is he?'

He placed him carefully on the pavement and the puppy bravely limped a few steps, holding his right front paw up.

'I'm really sorry, Serge,' I said. 'He was too quick for me. I just couldn't catch him.'

'He's hurt his leg,' said Serge. 'You don't think he's broken it, do you?' He was distraught.

'Oh God, I can't stand it! He's going to be a cripple all his life.' He picked up the little animal and clutched him to his chest. The pressure must have hurt because Robespierre gave another little cry of pain.

'Maybe he's just bruised his leg,' said Helen. 'It might not be broken.'

Serge put him down again and we watched him limp in circles and widdle on a piece of grass. When he'd finished we examined him under the interior light in the van.

'No, I think he *has* broken his leg,' Serge said hollowly.

We drove in silence back to Serge's hotel and carried the puppy up to his room. When Serge put him down on the carpet he tried to walk but fell forward again, clearly in great pain.

'We ought to get him to a vet,' said Helen.

'We'll never find a surgery open at this time of night,' said Serge. He was close to tears.

'I'm so sorry,' I said. 'I should have caught him.'

'How could you see him in the dark?' said Serge. 'It wasn't your fault, Johnny. Don't blame yourself.'

'What can we do?' said Helen. 'We can't just leave him in agony like this.'

The little animal was sitting looking up at us with one front paw held off the ground and a pleading expression on his face. It was pitiful.

'The holy water!' exclaimed Serge. 'I left the bottles in the van.'

He ran off to get them and we looked at each other with raised eyebrows.

'That won't do anything,' said Helen.

'No, but let's just humour him, eh?' I said.

He returned excitedly with the blue plastic bottles, unscrewed the top of one and poured some of the holy water into a dish.

Robespierre hobbled painfully over and began lapping it up.

'See, he was thirsty,' said Serge, 'the poor little chap.'

The puppy finished the water and ran his tongue round his chops as if relishing every last drop.

Serge poured some of the holy water into his hand and sploshed it on the dog's chest, rubbing it gently into his front legs.

'You've got to have faith,' he said, 'when you want something wonderful to happen.'

Serge seemed like an unlikely convert to the efficacy of holy water. And I was dubious that its powers extended to mending a broken leg.

Robespierre sat back on his haunches and looked up at us. The holy water didn't appear to be having any effect.

'We should get him to the vet first thing,' I said. 'If his leg is broken it will need setting.'

I was about to suggest we all turn in when the animal stood up on all fours and shook himself. He walked confidently across the room, turned and gave a little bark.

'He wants his dinner,' said Serge. 'In all the excitement I've forgotten to give him his dinner.'

'But did you see him?' said Helen eagerly. 'He's not limping. He walked perfectly. The holy water – it's worked!'

'My God! You're right!' said Serge. 'Look, he's fine now.'

He opened a tin of dog food. When Robespierre smelled the meat he hopped around eagerly waiting for it to be dished up.

We stood over him, watching him tuck in. The change in his behaviour was astounding.

'The holy water has cured him,' said Serge. He picked up Robespierre and hugged him. 'It's a miracle!'

Helen and I lay in bed in our caravan in the dark talking. We were still filled with wonder, unable to sleep.

I said, 'Do you think that holy water really cured Robespierre?'

'Well, he did seem to suddenly get better.'

'But surely holy water only works in horror films? He could have just twisted his leg and his hunger made him forget the pain.'

'Maybe. But Serge is right – you've got to have faith when you want something wonderful to happen.'

'That was wonderful though, what happened there at the grotto tonight,' I said softly. 'I've been trying to explain it to myself but my brain just goes numb. I can't seem to get to grips with it.'

'I'm pleased we came,' she said. 'I don't want to move back to England now and I feel like life's not so bad after all.'

I was relieved to hear it.

'I'm glad,' I said. 'Perhaps that's the miracle of Lourdes.'

'And I've changed my mind about Serge,' she said. 'He loves his dog so much. He's not so bad either.'

'Hitler loved his German shepherd dogs,' I said, '... and he was a vegetarian.'

'Everyone always says that,' she said.

Early next morning, when we arrived at Serge's hotel, he was already up, tucking into his coffee and croissants.

'How's Robespierre?' asked Helen.

'He's on top form,' said Serge. 'One hundred per cent. He broke off the end of a croissant, dipped it in jam and Robespierre took it daintily and licked the tips of Serge's fingers.

We joined him for breakfast and I couldn't help noticing that he was shaved and scrubbed. He was positively glowing. Maybe it was just the access to the hotel shower and free toilet facilities, but he seemed more wholesome somehow, quite unlike his usual scruffy old self.

'And what about you?' I said. 'You're all right?'

'I'm more than all right, Johnny, I'm a new man.'

There was something about his eyes. They were shining with a kind of zealous fervour.

'After all that happened last night,' he said, 'our wonderful experience at the grotto and the miracle healing of my darling Robespierre, I've decided the time has come to turn over a new leaf.'

We must have both looked incredulous because he seemed hurt.

'No, truthfully, you may not believe me but I'm going to change my ways. When I think about some of the things I've done in my life I'm embarrassed. I've messed up every decent relationship I've ever had.'

'What about Regine?' I said. 'You two love each other.'

'I haven't told anyone yet; she dumped me a while back for a rich widower from Paris who's taken her and the children away and given them the lifestyle they deserve... not sweating over sewing machines churning out fake teddies.'

'God, I'm so sorry,' I said.

'Yes, well, let's face it, I deserved it. I've been unfaithful, dishonest. I've lied and cheated everybody.'

'It's not so easy, the life of a *brocanteur*,' said Helen, comfortingly.

'Yes, sometimes you have to be a bit tough to survive,' I said.

'No, it's no good making excuses. I've acted like a swine. I'm ashamed of myself.'

'Steady on, Serge,' I said. 'I'm not sure if I can cope with you turning into a goody-goody.'

'I'm serious, Johnny. I lose Regine and now this little miracle with Robespierre. It's a sign. I've seen the light. I'm giving up my old selfish ways. I'm turning over a new leaf.'

Dawn was breaking when we finished breakfast and set off in Serge's van for the village where the *brocante* market was being held. Robespierre snuggled up on Helen's lap in the front. He seemed absolutely fine now.

We began setting up our stall in the village square.

'I'll just take Robespierre for a pee-pee,' said Serge. 'See if I can pick up any bargains.'

The sun was rising over the rooftops, taking the morning chill out of the air, and we got so absorbed in unpacking our stock and serving customers that I forgot all about him. I was thinking about fetching a mid-morning coffee from the cafe opposite when there was a commotion from inside: raised voices and then angry shouting.

The door burst open and two bodies came flying out, locked together in mortal combat. It wasn't the sort of fighting you see in the films, either. They were rolling in the dirt, twisting ears, banging heads on the ground, biting and gouging. A couple of stallholders waded in to break it up. They pulled the combatants apart.

'It's Serge!' said Helen incredulously. 'I hope he's not hurt.'

We rushed forward to see, but the fight was over. Serge staggered back leaving his adversary lying on the pavement groaning. He wiped a dribble of blood from his nose with the back of his hand. His hair was roughed up and his face was grimy. He looked more like his scruffy old self again.

When his opponent turned over and pulled himself to his knees I recognised him immediately. It was Serge's gun-running pal Bruno the Basque and surprisingly he appeared to have got the worst of it. He climbed unsteadily to his feet. One eye was swelling up and he had a nasty graze on his forehead. He shook himself and glared at Serge as if he was considering having another go. A couple of his burly cronies hovered in the background, unsure of what to do. Then they helped him to his feet. Bruno looked sullenly around at the crowd, thought better of it, and turned on his heel and slunk off.

'My God, Serge,' said Helen. 'Are you all right?'

'Yeah, I'm fine,' he said, smiling a lopsided grin.

We followed him back into the cafe, where a petite, neatly dressed woman was holding Robespierre. Serge thanked her, picked him up and hugged him.

The owner appeared to have safeguarded Serge's glass of Ricard. He topped it up and gave Serge a wink. 'This one's on the house, *mon ami*.'

'What was that all about?' I asked. 'How come you're always getting into scraps with Bruno the Basque? I thought you two were supposed to be friends.'

He spluttered in his drink and coughed spatters of Ricard onto the counter. 'We were… once,' he said. 'I'd decided to ignore the incident of the lamp – you know, the one he stole from me at the chateau? But he just pushed my good nature too far and took advantage. He poked fun at me and, what's worse, he poked fun at my Robespierre here.' He stroked the puppy's ears and kissed him on the top of the head.

'I was telling him about the holy water and how it had cured Robespierre's broken leg. But he simply laughed and began mocking us. I saw red and went for him. I just couldn't help myself.'

'Sounds like he asked for it,' I said.

'He was goading me,' said Serge. 'I'll kill him next time.'

I was wondering what had happened to the new man who'd turned over a new leaf this morning, but decided not to comment. Deep down, though, I think I was glad to have the old Serge back.

17

CAMPING

The sign read 'CAMPING – SITE DE NATURISME.'

'Oh goody, a nature reserve,' I said to Helen. 'Let's camp here.'

We were on our way back from Lourdes and had decided to stop off for the night.

'Yes, this'll do. Let's go in,' she said. 'It'll be dark soon.'

Serge pulled alongside in his van. He had a big grin on his face. He got out and came over.

'This looks like a nice place, Johnny. I've always wanted to go *à poil*. Let's stay here.' He winked at Helen.

'What does he mean?' said Helen.

'I've no idea,' I said.

The camp looked pleasant enough: neat rows of cypresses with wooden chalets and in the distance tennis courts and a swimming pool.

There was a notice pointing to the '*Accueil*' (Reception). 'Serge and I will go and book us in,' I said.

As we walked across the freshly cut grass, the place seemed empty. No caravans or tents or holidaymakers about. If this had been England I'd have been surprised, but in France it wasn't unheard of. The holiday season had just finished on the last weekend of August and now it was deserted. It's only throughout July and August that campsites get packed to bursting as the French holiday *en masse*.

We approached the wooden 'Reception' hut and Serge knocked loudly on the door. A big brown dog appeared out of the gloom and began to bark loudly at us. It bared its teeth and looked ferocious.

'Let's forget about booking in,' said Serge stepping back. 'There doesn't seem to be anyone about. I saw the toilet blocks on the way over. If we bag a couple of pitches we can avail ourselves of all the facilities. If the owners don't show up we can sneak off in the morning and no one will be any the wiser.'

The dog was emitting deep, threatening growls. Serge was foolhardy enough to get down on one knee and try his kissy-kissy sound. The animal's hackles came up and it made a sudden bound forward. Serge leaped up and we made a rapid retreat, looking back fearfully. The dog watched us go, barking in triumph.

Back at our caravan, Helen cooked vegetarian sausages and mash. We sat down together, squashed up round the galley table. When we told Serge there was no meat in the sausages he didn't believe us. 'It's not bad,' he said, although I knew he'd decided we were completely mad for not eating meat. He cut up some bits and fed them to Robespierre.

'Robespierre likes them, anyway,' he said. 'But I don't think he's ready to become a vegetarian just yet.'

It was growing dark outside and there was still no sign of anybody about. Serge's eyelids were heavy and he stifled a yawn.

'We've got some blankets; you can sleep on the floor in the caravan if you like,' said Helen. I knew she hoped he'd say no – I didn't think she liked him *that* much.

'No, I'll be fine in the front of the van,' he said. 'I'm shagged out. I'm going to sleep like a log.'

I made him take some extra blankets in case it grew cold in the night. Marcel freezing to death in his van at Bordeaux had made more of an impression on me than I realised. Serge thanked me, shouted *'Dormez bien!'* and we heard his van door slam shut.

We must have both passed out as soon as our heads hit the pillows because the next thing I knew it was morning and the sun was streaming in through the caravan skylight. I decided to take an early shower and shave. As I tiptoed past Serge's van I was amazed at how loud his snoring was; classic long snorks followed by long drawn-out whistles like I'd only ever heard in *Popeye* cartoons before.

The cold snap had passed and it was a balmy morning. I was warm enough in just a T-shirt, shorts and sandals. As I exited the toilet block, drying my hair with my towel, I glanced across the campsite towards the tennis courts and immediately did a double take. My eyes were met by a sight reminiscent of the naturist magazine *Health and Efficiency*, circa 1950. Two young maidens divest of every stitch of clothing save sneakers and white socks were bouncing a multicoloured beach ball in the air, their naked bodies glowing in the clear morning light.

Slightly stunned, I staggered on towards our caravan to be confronted by an even more unsettling sight: a whole family of nudists coming down the gravel driveway. I looked around for an escape route but realised I could not avoid them. They were coming towards me – a naked father and two children with his nude wife bringing up the rear. The man was doing what I can now identify as the 'Naturist's Saunter', a gentle, strolling gait, leaning back to allow his whole body the full benefit of the sun's healing rays. As they drew level I managed a smile and wished them *'Bonjour'*.

Strangely, I felt embarrassed for being overdressed.

'It's warm,' I said, looking him in the eye, trying not to let my eyes be seen to drop to the 'naughty bits'.

'Mais oui,' he replied, *'beau temps.'* He sauntered off, followed closely by his bare-bottomed family.

I half-stumbled, half-ran back to our caravan to tell Helen the shocking news.

'This isn't a nature reserve, it's a nudist camp!' I yelled. 'The sun's brought them all out. It's the opposite to vampires.'

She just laughed.

'No, it's true, honestly.'

'Oh well, never mind,' she said. 'We'll just have to brazen it out. We've run out of water. Could you fill our plastic tank?'

'How can I go out there?' I said.

'Try it, you might like it. Just strip off and stop being so sensitive.'

'What, go out there in the nuddy?'

'Why not?'

I was taken aback. I know Helen stripped off at every chance in the garden but I had to convince myself I could cope with this. I pondered for a minute.

'OK, I'll do it,' I said.

I divested myself of my shorts, pants and T-shirt and set off. But I felt strangely eccentric hefting the empty polythene tank with fresh air circulating freely round parts that were usually hidden away. I peeked into the front of Serge's van just to assure myself he was asleep. Happily he was still snoring loudly, dead to the world.

As I walked along the gravel path headed for the water taps I felt myself slip automatically into the 'Naturist's Saunter', turning my naked body and leaning back to catch the sun's rays. I was beginning to feel I could pull this off. I looked the part and I actually felt like a real nudist – enough of one anyway to allay all suspicions.

I looked around in vain for evidence of other naturists, but there was no one about. The beach ball girls had vanished and there was no sign of the nude family.

As I filled my water tank I inadvertently splashed cold water on my private parts and jumped back in shock. I was starting to realise just how uncomfortable performing seemingly simple day-to-day functions could be without clothes on. When I staggered back with the full tank Helen couldn't stop laughing. 'You might as well empty our chemical loo while you're at it,' she giggled.

Yes, why not? There was nothing to be afraid of. I was starting to get into the swing of this nudist lark. Everyone was equal in the buff. It was somehow invigorating and liberating at the same time.

I set off ready for the task in hand when from behind I heard: 'Hey, Johnny, how's it hanging?'

I turned round, surprised. Serge had come up behind me. He was stark-bollock-naked. And he had a big smug grin on his face. But what struck me most was how amazingly hirsute he was. So much so that he didn't really need any clothes at all. It was an uncalled for and slightly repulsive revelation.

'So that's what *à poil* means?' I said.

'Yes, of course, Johnny. I thought you knew. Mind if I join you? I fancy a shower.'

'OK, certainly,' I said, trying to act normally. We set off up the path with me carrying the plastic Portaloo and Serge walking beside me with a towel over his shoulder.

'It's turned out nice again,' I said, trying not to look at his hairy body. 'Much warmer than yesterday.' It felt like a scene from *Carry on Camping*.

'Beautiful,' he said. 'And we'll soon get nice and bronzed, won't we?'

I couldn't help noticing he was doing the 'Naturist's Saunter', leaning back to catch the sun. Was this really his first visit to a nudist camp?

As we approached the toilet block we came face to face with a couple of builders wearing their traditional blue overalls and a woman I guessed to be an architect, examining plans spread out on a table. They were all fully clothed and the two of us were now in the unenviable reversed role of being stark naked. They ignored us, heads down, discussing what I presumed was to be some type of new building.

The woman looked up and smiled broadly at me. '*Bonjour...*' (and then I could have sworn she stared pointedly at my private parts) '*... m'sieu!*'

She glanced at Serge, appeared slightly appalled and looked quickly away.

The two builders gawped at us and one of them raised his eyebrows and smiled almost conspiratorially. As Serge and I entered the toilet block I realised he probably thought we were a gay couple on holiday together. My face was on fire. I wanted to tell them we were neither homosexuals nor nudists. We were in fact impostors who had snuck in undetected under false pretences.

As I emptied our Portaloo, I could hear Serge singing to himself in the shower, puffing and blowing like a grampus. I waited and he came out steaming, rubbing himself with his towel and making no attempt at modesty, like we were two pals up at the YMCA.

I looked out of the door hesitantly, dreading having to pass the builders and the woman again in such a vulnerable state. But I needn't have worried. They were climbing into a smart car and driving off.

Then, surprisingly, as we re-emerged, the world appeared to have reverted back to its 'naked as nature intended' state. There were nude couples wandering hand in hand, the man I had seen earlier with his wife and family reappeared and there were other naturists cavorting about bursting with health. Bare skin was in vogue again.

I ambled back with Serge towards our caravan, feeling quite at ease. We were managing to pull off this naturist lark. It wasn't as hard as I had imagined. All you had to do was keep a clear head, try not to panic and avoid any erotic thoughts that could lead to an embarrassing arousal situation.

As we approached our caravan I saw Helen at the window laughing hysterically before ducking down out of sight.

18

PIRATES AND VIOLINS

The room was packed to the rafters and buzzing like an all-night party. Dealers pushed through to bag a place, greeting each other warmly and shaking hands. Women were kissed ardently on both cheeks and pleasantries exchanged. In this *salle des ventes* (auction room) it was hard to imagine these same dealers would be fighting like hyenas to outbid each other once the sale started.

It was a couple of weeks after our visit to Lourdes and Serge had persuaded me that a six-hour drive deep into the heart of the Auvergne on a buying trip would be worth it.

'They're still living in the Dark Ages over there and you can pick up good old rustic furniture for nothing... they're practically giving it away.'

I was hoping – probably in vain – that he still had some vestiges of the new man left in him, so decided to accept his offer. After all, he'd been right about the Mickey Mouse cheque.

The countryside had been stunning but the trip a fraught one. My van had begun to play up in a most alarming manner. The accelerator stuck and the engine raced, sending us hurtling down a steep hill into a sleepy village, careering dangerously from side to side as I fought desperately to regain control. When I eventually managed to stop in neutral with the engine screaming we climbed out like Laurel and Hardy, looking baffled. Serge managed to fix it more by luck than judgement, but the trouble kept recurring and we needed to get to a garage and have the problem sorted out by a proper mechanic.

I was worrying about it as we pushed our way through the throng of dealers trying to get a look at the furniture.

My experience of salerooms in Britain had left me unprepared for what went on in France. Helen had told me but I hadn't really believed her. Here, as in most French auctions, there was no catalogue with descriptions of the items and their lot number. You had to remember what you wanted to buy and wait until it came up. There appeared to be no rhyme nor reason as to when goods were picked out to go under the hammer and the sale verged on the farcical. This was in no small part due to the mother and daughter team who ran the place. They had a passable double act going between them which would not have seemed out of place on the variety stage.

The daughter was perched high up behind a desk on a dais, while the mother helped out the teenage porter, moving round the hall, showing off special items, shouting comments and cracking jokes. She was sixty if she was a day and fancied herself as something of a femme fatale.

She decided to model a fur coat that was up for sale, slinking down the aisles like Brigitte Bardot to wolf whistles from the crowd, fluttering her eyelids and throwing lewd wisecracks at a dealer half her age she had the hots for. The daughter, meanwhile, who was trying to run the auction, periodically halted the proceedings to threaten her mother with her gavel, telling her to act her age and stop fooling around.

I felt a nudge in the ribs. 'Oi-oi, mate. 'Ow's it goin'?'

I turned to look into the deeply lined, weather-beaten face of Reg, an English dealer I'd seen around.

'Bleedin' froggy farce, eh? What *are* they playing at?'

He raised his eyebrows and they disappeared under his shaggy mop of hair. He'd stuck with the same Rolling Stones style all his life, only now it was streaked with grey and was perhaps even more unruly than it had been in the sixties. He lifted his arm to shout out a bid and revealed a muscled forearm covered in tattoos. Reg's tattoos weren't the fake tribal designs of today's youth. Besides stylised bluebirds like the one I had he sported dripping daggers, tombstones, staring skulls and tributes to Jimi Hendrix and the Grateful Dead.

'I see you've got your froggy mate with you,' he said, nodding at Serge, whom he viewed with a mixture of amusement and contempt.

'Is his surname really Bastarde? Unbelievable! Is that why you hang out with him, just for a laugh?'

I ignored the remark but felt slightly chastened. Despite his bigoted bluff exterior, Reg was nobody's fool. I couldn't help feeling he had an uncanny insight into what made us tick.

He play-punched Serge, who grinned and gave his hair a tug. I knew Serge was impressed by him. He referred to him as *Le Pirate* and recognised a fellow jovial degenerate when he saw one.

The mother and daughter team were well into their stride now. The daughter had knocked down an ormolu clock to someone at the back of the room and a squabble broke out. The dealer who thought he had won the bid began to argue vociferously when he realised the clock was going to a rival. Voices were raised in anger and a certain amount of bad-tempered jostling began. Any sensible auctioneer would have nipped a dispute like this in the bud, cancelled the sale and restarted the bidding. But the daughter joined in the fight, pointing and screaming, insisting that her decision was final. The mother seized the opportunity to back the loser and a slanging match developed between the pair of them.

Serge sided with one of the dealers and, to my horror, began shouting disparaging remarks about the daughter's competence.

She exploded in a temper tantrum. 'Any cheek from you, Bastarde, and I'll have you thrown out!' Her face was bright red. She looked like she might burst a blood vessel.

The mother jumped straight in on Serge's side, defending him and berating her daughter. She winked and smiled at Serge and I got the distinct impression they might have had some history together.

'Seems like you're notorious even round here,' I said.

He chuckled and nodded.

'Better go easy though,' I said. 'We haven't managed to buy anything yet.'

'Don't worry about that, Johnny. I've got the piston, friends in the right places. Me and the mother, we had a bit of a thing going a while back. She'll see me right.'

So my suspicions were correct. He'd been her 'boyfriend'. The crafty old devil!

The daughter calmed down and began auctioning off a box of books. But the mother insisted on helping her, picking them out one by one, thumbing through and choosing passages she thought might interest us, reading out loud as if we were pupils in a class. There were a few yawns and shuffling of feet but no one complained or shouted 'Get on with it!' as they would have done in an English auction room.

I decided this was the time to nip to the loo but it seemed like everyone had the same idea because when I got there the place was packed. As I shuffled behind the line of men waiting to use the stinking urinal, I was thinking about how I was going to get the van fixed, and absent-mindedly looking at the back of the neck of the chap in front of me. He turned his head slightly and I noticed the end of a livid scar running from one ear down across his throat. Where had I seen that scar recently? It was hardly the sort of thing you could forget. Then it hit me: it was Bruno the Basque! Surely he couldn't have followed us out here intent on revenge.

I changed my mind about taking a piss and pushed my way out, through the corridor and into the street.

Breathing in the fresh air I fought to get a grip. I hadn't realised what an ugly impression Bruno had made on me. Reg was leaning against a wall in the shade.

'What's up with you?' he said. 'You look like you've seen a ghost.'

I leaned back beside him.

'I hear you've had a spot of trouble with your old *camion.*'

I was only mildly surprised that he knew. Although his grasp of French was limited he was a sheer genius at conversing with signs and exaggerated facial expressions, and I'd seen him 'chatting' with Serge earlier. He didn't miss a trick and knew far more about what was going on than I did.

'It is playing up a bit,' I said. 'I'm going to have to check it into a garage.'

'You can stay at my place tonight if you like.'

'I didn't know you lived locally.'

'Nah, I don't, but I've got me caravan parked on the gypo site outside town.'

Erk! The gypo site outside town. I didn't like the sound of that.

'Surely gypos... I mean Gypsies... don't like non-*gitans* on their sites?'

'Nah, that's a load of bollocks. If they don't like it they can get stuffed,' he said gruffly.

'I don't want to put you to any trouble. I'm sure we can find a *pension* or something here.'

'No trouble at all, mate. I've already rung the wife and told her to sort out an evening meal for us.'

That was it then. There was no argument. It was a fait accompli. When I told Serge about Reg's offer he was delighted, especially about the free meal part.

'*Voilà*, and *Le Pirate* has a charming wife. Our luck's in again. You know, Johnny, your English women are very sexy. When I was in the army I seduced the wives of many English tourists. It worked every time. I was young and handsome and dashing in my army uniform.' How many times had I heard that one?! Looking at him now, squat and swarthy like a toad, it didn't seem possible. Had I imagined him jiving with Angelique that night I got drunk during La Fête de la Musique? He had a twinkle in his eye and a cheeky grin. Maybe he was irresistible to some women.

I was about to ask him if he knew his old pal Bruno the Basque was here, when bidding started on the country furniture and the moment passed. I even managed to buy a couple of pieces for a reasonable price and decided to nip out and find a garage to fix the van. I knew from experience in France that if you drive a French vehicle you can normally get any repairs done speedily and efficiently in the smaller local garages. I found one owned by a pair of twin brothers who looked like they had stepped out of a *Tintin* comic book, all berets and matching blue overalls. They seemed pleased to get the work and promised to have the problem sorted out before lunch the following day.

I returned to the saleroom, expecting to find Serge waiting for me, but he had vanished. A few dealers were loading their vans and I asked around without much success. Someone said they'd seen him with *'Monsieur le Rock 'n' Roll Anglais'*, but didn't know where they'd gone.

I wandered into town, feeling lost and sorry for myself. I was stuck deep in the heart of the Auvergne, abandoned, hungry and alone. As I walked up the main street imagining what I'd say to Serge when I caught up with him I was struck by an incongruous sight – a flashing pink neon sign bearing the legend 'Tivoli Bar' over a red-painted doorway. I was musing that this was more the type of sign you'd come across in a seedy quarter of somewhere like Paris or Marseille than a sleepy little town in the Auvergne when there was a sudden commotion inside – maniacal laughter mixed with apoplectic yells backed by a chorus of high-spirited out-of-tune singing.

I looked up and down the peaceful street. Two women were chatting in front of the butcher's. A couple of old boys were sitting sipping Pernods outside a small cafe.

The door to the Tivoli Bar burst open and Reg and Serge staggered out, arms round each other, singing at the tops of their voices – a drunken version of 'Angie' by the Rolling Stones. They caroused past me oblivious, before Serge did a double take and swung round in surprise.

'Eh, Johnny, where you been? I was looking for you.'

He put one arm round my shoulder. In the other he was holding a violin, dangling it by the fretboard like a club.

'I thought you'd deserted me,' I said, relieved, and unable to recall any of the horrible things I'd intended to say to him.

'Desert you? No, never, Johnny! *Le Pirate* and me, we've been making *la fête*.'

'I've sorted the van out,' I said.

'Good, good.'

He didn't give a shit.

'What's that?' I asked.

'This? *Le violon*?' He tapped the side of his nose with his forefinger. 'It's the reason we're celebrating.'

Reg was standing with a goofy grin on his face. What were the pair of them on? I knew Reg wasn't averse to a bit of substance abuse, and Serge would be loath to refuse any free samples. It was the only way they could have got so wasted in such a short period of time.

'Come on, let's go mad and have a good time,' said Serge, steering me towards the door.

Reg threw back his head, opened his mouth and brayed out: *'Angie! Angie! La-la-la-la-la-la-laaaaa!'*

Surprisingly, the bar was packed and as we pushed through I recognised most of the customers as dealers from the auction room. I scanned the crowd uneasily, wondering if Bruno the

Basque was among them. We found a corner table and Serge thrust the violin into my hand.

'Protect that with your life, Johnny.'

He staggered off to the bar and returned with a bottle of champagne and glasses which he plonked down before us. He tottered off, chuckling to himself.

Reg helped himself to a glass, downing it in one swig. He leaned over conspiratorially and grasped my knee as he took a deep drag on his cigarette. 'I'd guard that violin with your life like he says if I were you, mate.'

'It's worth a lot is it?'

'It's only a bleedin' Stradivarius, my man; it'll cost you four pound ten.' He erupted with a roar of laughter which turned into a coughing fit. I thumped him on the back as he fought for breath.

'Poor old Benny Hill, eh?' he gasped. 'A bloody funny bloke killed off by feminists. Crying shame.'

He wiped the tears from his eyes.

'But seriously though, Serge had to fight the gypos to get that thing. He's got some bottle that little pal of yours, I'll give him that. I thought those pikeys were going to shiv him at one point.'

I didn't like the sound of this. Could they have got into so much trouble in such a short time?

'It was a set-up,' said Reg. 'Serge told me the whole story. That old girl, the mother, had phoned him to tip him off that a valuable Italian violin was coming up in their next auction. They planned to pull a fast one together and swing the sale.'

So that was why Serge had wanted me to drive him all this way out into the back of beyond. Rustic furniture my arse!

'Only the word went round,' said Reg, 'and every pikey within a hundred-mile radius turns up and tries to get in on the act. Those gypos know every con in the book and when the violin was knocked down to Serge for such a low bid they went bananas.'

'How do you mean?' I said. I was thinking about Bruno the Basque.

'A gang of them were waiting outside when we left. Great big beefy broad-shouldered blokes with meaty hands and bellies like hippopotamuses. They barred our way and I thought we'd had it. But Serge faced them down – walked straight through calm as you like. I was sure we were in for some real trouble, but I've seen no sign of them since.'

'Was one of them a horrible character with a big livid scar round his neck?'

'Yeah, as it happens, there was a bloke like that. Nasty piece of work. Had a right go at Serge, he did.'

'That's Bruno the Basque. He and Serge were mates when they were boys, but they fell out in a big way.'

I told him the story of the chateau and the Gallé lamp. He was fascinated.

'They're worth a fortune, those Gallé lamps are.'

'I don't think it was genuine,' I said. 'It looked like repro to me.'

I examined the violin in my hand. It seemed particularly unprepossessing. Could it have really made Bruno and a load of Gypsies go bananas? I turned it at an angle to the light and looked in through the S-shaped holes. There was a faded yellow label stuck inside. I could just make out the lettering. Reg hadn't been joking.

'See, you didn't believe me,' he said. 'It *is* a bleedin' Stradivarius.'

'Yes, but there are loads of violins with the label marked Stradivarius stuck inside.' I said. 'Doesn't mean to say it's genuine.'

'So do you think this violin could be the same thing as that Gallé lamp? A fake worth fuck all?'

'Not necessarily. Some of them were made by skilled associates or sons of Stradivarius himself, apparently. I'm not an expert but this could be worth a few bob I suppose.

Serge reckons it's worth a fortune. He's going to flog it and retire. That's why we're celebrating.'

At that moment Serge reappeared and I handed him back the violin. 'This was what it was all about then?' I said.

He looked at me as if he didn't understand.

'The violin. That's why we came all this way. It wasn't for the cheap country furniture at all.'

He gave me a sheepish grin. 'So *Le Pirate* has given away my little secret, eh?'

'You could have let me in on it. I wouldn't have minded.'

'I wasn't sure about it, honestly, Johnny. I was working on a tip-off. And you did get some good stuff too, didn't you?'

What was the use? I wasn't surprised he'd duped me yet again.

Reg stood up shakily, clapped his hands and rubbed them together like a drunken Master of Ceremonies. 'Maybe we should make a move, lads. The wife will have dinner ready and will be wondering where we are. Don't want to keep her waiting, do we?'

We followed him out to his van and I managed to squeeze in between some heavy pieces of brown furniture.

'You all right in the back there?' asked Reg, as we rattled along. It reminded me of similar situations I'd been in with the John Dummer Blues Band in the late sixties after a gig, driving pissed on our way back to some cheap hotel for the night. Only then I'd been as legless as the rest of them. Now I was older, wiser and stone-cold sober. Every time Reg broke into a chorus of 'Angie' and swerved out of the path of an oncoming vehicle I nearly shat myself.

We pulled up in a cloud of dust at a Gypsy encampment on the outskirts of town, narrowly missing a surly bunch of bored teenagers. They eyed us coldly, pulling on their fags as we parked beside Reg's grubby, dog-eared English caravan, which stuck out like a sore thumb among the shiny Lord Munsterlands the Gypsies favoured.

I'd never been onto a Gypsy site, just driven past them, but this one was idyllic with views across open meadows thick with wild flowers. All around were spanking new Mercedes white vans and spotless, glittering caravans, each with its own satellite dish. Were the Gypsies somehow a lot more successful at this *brocante* lark than we were? Clearly they were. How did they manage it? I looked around with some trepidation. I half expected to see Bruno the Basque and a bunch of his cronies coming to get us.

Reg let out a drunken yell, took a last swig of champagne and lobbed the bottle into the bushes.

We were greeted by his wife, who I couldn't help noticing had a half-smoked spliff sticking out of the corner of her mouth. She was rangy, with straw-coloured hair, and introduced herself as Rita. I got a strong taste of alcohol mixed with pot when she planted a big wet kiss full on my mouth. In her heyday she might have been an attractive woman. But I got the impression that, like Reg's caravan, she had become a bit dog-eared over the years. My hunch that she might not be at her best in the charm department at the moment was soon to be proved correct.

The caravan reeked sickly sweet. She seated us at a pull-down table while she staggered about in the cramped space, clattering pots and pans and rattling drawers of cutlery. She plonked down a bowl of some concoction which looked yellow and cheesy and strangely unappetising.

Reg lolled forward, barely aware of what was happening. How he'd managed to drive the van was beyond me.

'A little something I made earlier,' slurred Rita, leaning on the table for support. 'Cauliflower cheese. Hope you like cauliflower cheese. My Reggie loves it.' She ladled a great steaming lump onto her husband's plate, dripping runny cheese across the table. Serge watched her every move avidly. I could tell he found her anarchic manner seductive. He was clutching his violin to his chest like a kid with a favourite cuddly toy, smiling secretly to himself.

The cheesy smell galvanised Reg into action. He appeared to re-enter his slumping body, straightening up and attacking the food, spooning it into his mouth. Rita watched him indulgently.

'He does love his cauliflower cheese, my Reggie does.'

Serge took a mouthful of his and pulled a strange face. He looked like he couldn't decide whether to swallow or spit it out.

Rita noticed. 'Whatsa matter, lovey, don't you like it? Oh cripes! Silly me. I forgot the baked beans, didn't I.' She fetched a steaming saucepan and doled some out onto our plates.

Serge looked at the bright orangey goo as if he couldn't believe his eyes.

'You'll want some HP sauce with that,' said Rita. She produced a bottle with a dried brown collar and whacked it with the palm of her hand, sending dollops flying in all directions.

'What do you think of this then, Serge?' I said. 'Traditional English grub.'

He was put on the spot. He couldn't face it but didn't want to offend Rita. He swallowed with difficulty and wiped his lips with the back of his hand. He looked about to vomit. 'I've just got to nip out for a moment,' he said. 'I won't be long.' He stumbled out the door, still clutching his violin.

'Sweet little bloke,' said Rita. 'What did he say?'

'He's just off to the loo,' I said.

'What's 'is name again?'

'Serge,' I said. 'Serge Bastarde.'

'Never,' she said. 'Is his name really Bastarde?' She had a fit of the giggles. She appeared as incredulous about it as Reg was.

'It's not that uncommon a surname in France,' I said.

'Blimey, fancy that,' she spluttered.

Reg had polished off his cauliflower cheese and was helping himself to the last of the beans, liberally coated with HP sauce. The meal appeared to have completely revived him. He was his old self again. He grinned at me.

'All right then, mate?'

'Brilliant,' I said, trying to appear enthusiastic. The food actually tasted fine, although baked beans and cauliflower cheese held no terrors for me. I'd been brought up on the sticky stuff. It was hard to comprehend how the French saw these dishes as strange and somehow exotic. Christmas pudding always came top of the chart of Bizarre British Dishes, but baked beans were up there somewhere, probably in the top five.

'Where's Serge?' asked Reg.

'He's gone to the loo, I think.' I was beginning to worry about him. What if Bruno and his thugs knew he was here? He wouldn't stand a chance out there on his own.

'Feeling a bit Tom and Dick is he?'

'He's hardly touched his dinner,' said Rita. She had produced a 'cubey', a big square plastic bottle of cheap red wine, and was sloshing a glass full. She knocked it back and poured herself another.

'Those gypo kids are being a right nuisance, babe,' she said, taking a last drag on the tip of the joint, stubbing it out on Reg's plate and dropping the end into his glass. 'There's one of them fancies me. He keeps leering and lurking around. Gives me the creeps, so he does.'

'Do you want me to knock him out?' asked Reg.

Rita let out a cackle.

He leaned over and looked out the caravan window. 'Point him out to me. I'll go and do him.'

'I think he's the sprog of that Antonio what's-'is-name, the one who reckons he's the King of the Gypsies,' she said.

'Bloody gypos!' said Reg, flopping back. 'I used to do a fair old trade with them. But they can't get the good stolen stuff anymore. What's the use? They're not worth bothering with.' He began to help himself to the 'cubey' but stopped as the strains of a violin drifted in from outside. It was exquisitely played, a romantic air dripping with emotion. Reg put down his drink, leaned over, lifted the plastic net curtains and peered out of the window.

'That's nice,' said Rita. 'Fancy being able to play the violin like that.'

'He can't,' I said. 'Least, not as far as I know.'

As we listened the music segued unexpectedly into a jazzy blues. Whoever was playing certainly knew their stuff.

We left our meals and went outside where a little old man in shirtsleeves, waistcoat and a black trilby hat was playing the violin like a man possessed.

Serge was standing close by, watching spellbound. He wasn't sick after all. Tears welled in his eyes. His face was flushed with emotion.

The little old man finished the blues and began a flamenco, passionate and strutting at the same time. Serge swayed to the music, blinking back the tears. He smiled beatifically at us.

'See, listen to that. Fantastic! That's my violin that is. I knew it was a good one.'

The enormity of the moment hit us. We were jubilant. All three of us grabbed him and went into what I can only describe as a group hug, dancing with delight. Then, slightly embarrassed, we pulled back and clapped in time to the music.

When the flamenco finished, we broke into spontaneous applause. The man handed the violin to Serge, bowed to us, waved his hand with a flourish and walked off towards the other caravans with great dignity.

'Blimey, who was that bloke?' said Reg.

'He's a *gitan* violinist,' said Serge, his voice cracking.

'How did he get off the fag packet then?' said Reg. He looked at me like I'd appreciate the joke. I assumed he was referring to the picture of the romantic Gypsy with silver earrings on the old blue Gitanes cigarettes packet, and laughed knowingly.

'He couldn't half play that fiddle,' said Rita.

'He assured me my violin was a very rare find made by craftsmen,' said Serge. He was beginning to sound a bit smug.

We went back into the caravan where Serge waxed lyrical about what he intended to do with the fortune he was going to make when he sold his violin.

'I've always wanted to travel, Johnny,' he said. 'I think I'd like to see India. Maybe Egypt... the pyramids in the moonlight.'

I explained it all to Rita. 'What about a cruise?' she volunteered. 'A cruise would be nice.' I could tell she was viewing Serge in a new light. She leaned in closer and smiled seductively. He did have a certain attraction for some women. It was obvious to me now.

Reg turned the violin in his hands. 'It's a beauty, isn't it? And what a lovely tone it's got.' He placed it carefully on the table as if it were alive and delicate like a newborn baby. 'You done all right this time, mate.' He mimed an enthusiastic thumbs-up. 'Will you still talk to me when you're rich? I bet you won't want to know me.'

Serge had a dreamy look on his face, as if he'd won the lottery. Rita was cooing to him. 'You'll need someone to keep you company on your world tour, babe. I could do that for you... look after you and help you spend the money.' Her hand was on his knee. I wondered if Reg had noticed and how he'd react. I anticipated him punching Serge on the nose and the blood spurting.

But Reg was rubbing his fingers together in a miserly fashion and pulling a greedy face.

'I think maybe I'll retire,' said Serge. 'Take a break. Not retire exactly, but do all the things I've always wanted to do.

You know, live a lavish lifestyle, treat all my friends, throw big parties.'

I passed on these musings to Reg and Rita.

'Ah, bless,' said Rita.

'Yeah, good on you, mate,' said Reg. 'You enjoy yourself.' He lifted his glass to propose a toast. They knocked back the wine and laughed together.

The violin was on the table. I picked it up reverentially and examined it. I thought I'd memorise exactly what it was like just in case my luck changed and I came across another one worth a fortune. It'd never happen... but you just never knew. I looked in through the S-shaped holes.

'My God! Look at this. Read the label.'

I passed it to Reg, who took it and peered in through the slots.

'Blimey! It's clear as day... Made in China. They've done him. Someone's done a swapsy. It must have been that old fag packet bloke.

Serge was in a reverie. His head was leaning on Rita's bosom. He was smiling at her as she stroked the back of his neck.

Reg poked him hard and shouted at him.

'Look at this! They've conned you, you prat!'

Serge looked up guiltily. He thought Reg was attacking him for partaking of the pleasures of his wife. But Reg was pushing the violin at him, indicating inside.

Serge grasped the instrument and peered through the apertures. His eyes widened as he read the label. He couldn't believe it. He looked round in panic.

Then suddenly he was off and out the door, legging it across the site, disappearing through the caravans, shouting at people.

I went to follow and help the poor sod. But Reg stopped me.

'Don't bother, mate. He'll have to go some to catch that little bloke. That was a set-up, that was. He's got no chance. He and that violin will be long gone.'

Serge reappeared later, looking utterly dejected. He was muttering pathetically. 'Everyone denied that bloke existed. They said they'd heard nothing... no one like that here... They turned their backs on me.'

Rita helped him back into the caravan.

'Come on darlin', never mind, eh? You never finished your dinner and there's rhubarb and custard for afters.'

Serge gave her a wan smile.

19

RINGS AND ROMANCE

It was a baking hot afternoon but cool in our *atelier*, where I was antique-waxing a walnut country table. Helen was out at an auction and, apart from the gentle cooing of the pigeons in the nesting boxes on the barn wall and the distant purr of a tractor, all was calm and peaceful.

I looked out through the open door across the fields thick with maize that now completely surrounded us. The stalks rustled soothingly as a gentle breeze stirred the drying leaves. It was now fully grown and ready for the combine harvester. I was reminded of the line from the song 'Oh, What a Beautiful Morning' from the Rogers and Hammerstein musical, *Oklahoma,* in which the corn is described as being 'as high as an elephant's eye'. It possibly depended on the size of the elephant but we were now completely hidden in our own secret little world.

I recognised the throb of the tractor. It belonged to Mr Leglise, a sprightly eighty-five-year-old with a twinkle in his eye, one of our *agricole* neighbours, who wore wooden clogs, a blue cotton jacket and trousers and a beret in all weathers. When it was hot he left off the jacket and went barefoot, walking confidently across his land. He had a small farm across the way; a couple of lush meadows, one cow, a donkey and a small mongrel dog. The donkey was prone to letting fly intermittent loud braying cries at any hour of the day and night. It was driven into the meadows with the cow every morning to the accompaniment of frantic barking from the dog.

I had recently set up my drum kit in our caravan near the *atelier* and when I got the urge I would treat myself to a deeply satisfying thrash about on it just to keep my hand in. I was slightly worried that the loud sound of my abandoned workouts might annoy the neighbours, but when I stopped to wish Mr Leglise *'bonjour'* after one of my sessions, he assured me, 'The beat of the drums, I love it. It's full of life.' Anything that brought a bit of life and soul to the village appeared to be embraced wholeheartedly by one and all and I received no complaints, even though Helen assured me the sound was deafening.

Wednesday was market day in our local village and Mr Leglise never missed a get-together with all his octogenarian pals. I felt slightly envious of them sometimes when I passed the bar and saw them laughing uproariously together, knocking back glasses of Pernod. They were relaxed in one another's company and had probably known each other since their schooldays. I couldn't help comparing them to some of the sad-faced pensioners I'd seen hanging disconsolately around shopping malls in England. Where has our modern society gone wrong?

I discovered Mr Leglise was as prone to letting himself go and expressing himself as I was. On hot afternoons he would set up his gramophone outside his farmhouse and sing along to his collection of old 78 and 45 rpm records. He had a strong, rich baritone voice and the spirited sound of his singing would waft across the fields.

I half-expected to hear him start up now as I enjoyed waxing the walnut table, buffing it up and seeing the satisfying deep lustre of the wood as it began to shine. Ah, the small pleasures of furniture restoration. As I polished away I was thinking absent-mindedly about our trip last weekend into the Auvergne and wondering if we would ever discover who it was that nicked Serge's Stradivarius. My money was on Serge's old friend turned arch-enemy Bruno the Basque. I had a strong hunch he was the brains behind it.

I jumped involuntarily. Someone had crept up on me and pinched my bottom. Well, well… I wonder who? I turned to see Helen smiling wickedly.

'I thought you were at an auction,' I said, pleased to see her.

'I was, but the auctioneer stopped it early. She completely lost her temper because everything was going cheaply. She went berserk and threw us all out.'

'Good God! Why?'

'All the other dealers were at a funeral so there were only private buyers and me there. There weren't many bids and things were going ridiculously cheap, it was great. But she didn't like it and blew a fuse.'

I'd seen the woman auctioneer she was talking about and wasn't really surprised. She ran her sales like an ayatollah, punishing anyone who crossed her, regularly losing her temper and scolding dealers who stepped out of line.

'The funeral was of a married couple – *brocanteurs* who did the markets,' said Helen, 'and guess what – they were murdered!'

I was shocked. The local *Sud Ouest* newspaper carried hardly any crime stories. Murder was something that happened in New York, not here in Landes. Most murders were in other parts of France, although we did get some action with ETA (the outlawed Basque separatist group), being so near the Spanish border and the Pays Basque. The terrorists tended to be caught hiding in houses in Landes with stashes of arms and explosives. Recently the police had taken to stopping and searching cars on the quiet back roads, usually with an armed marksman with an automatic weapon stationed behind them to open fire on any suspect cars making a run for it.

Otherwise not much happened aside from the odd armed bank robbery, or the theft of wedding presents left in the house when the whole village was attending the church service and reception because the parents of the couple had placed an announcement of the happy day in the local paper. Our neighbours had even taken to hiring security guards to stop this occurring.

'Someone told me they were missing for weeks before their bodies were found in shallow graves in the woods,' said Helen.

'Really? I hadn't heard about it,' I said.

'Yes, well that's our problem; as foreigners we're a bit outside their world even though we speak French. It's like being in a little village in England where you're an outsider for years.'

'I'll ask about and maybe find out what happened tomorrow when I'm at Montauban,' I said. I was off in the early hours to do a two-day fair there and I could probably pick up on the gossip.

'Why don't we go together?' she said. 'The people at the town hall said there was room to park our caravan nearby if we wanted to.'

'That'd be even better. I'd like that.'

'Better get on with your restoration then… Or on second thoughts come in and make me a cup of tea. I'm dying of thirst.'

'Tea… tea? Is that your answer to it all?' I said jokingly.

'Yes,' she said, 'it is.'

The market square at Montauban was already thronged with white vans when we arrived. It was early in September but still hot and one of those shady sweet mornings under the plane trees before the full force of the sun begins to suck all the moisture out of the air. We parked our caravan overlooking the river and queued up to be allocated our pitch by *le placier* (the market supervisor). Once the van was in place we joined all the other traders in the local cafe for a coffee.

Montauban was a bit out of our area so I didn't recognise a lot of the faces. But Louis, my jazz-loving friend from Dax was there as usual and he came across and pumped my hand, glad to see us. We talked about the Marciac Jazz Festival, which is held every year in a little village in the Gers. He regularly rented a stall in the market for the two-week festival and sold collectors' records, esoteric T-shirts and memorabilia to the jazz fans. He hadn't taken a lot of money this year, but it was more like a labour of love for him.

'There's not many of the "greats" left alive now, John. It's sad, isn't it?'

I was agreeing and sympathising when I felt a dig in the ribs and turned to see Reg.

'Oi-oi, Johnny boy, we can't go on meeting like this.'

I was pleasantly surprised to see him again. Things were seldom boring when he was around. 'And you must be his wife, darlin',' he said, turning to Helen. 'Nice to meet you. Serge told me a bit about you, and Johnny 'ere never stops talking about you.'

'I didn't know you ever got over this way Reg,' I said, feeling slightly embarrassed.

'I don't as a rule. But it's been a bit quiet and I thought, why not? It's gonna be a scorcher today too by the looks of it. Good job I've got me caravan parked nearby so Rita can bring me drinks an' that.'

'That's a coincidence,' I said, 'because we've brought ours as well.'

'Great! We can all hang out together and have a laugh.' He nudged me. 'Watch out – here comes trouble.' He nodded towards the door where Serge was pushing his way through.

Reg put an imaginary violin under his chin and mimed playing it. When Serge saw what he was doing he threw me and Helen a pained look. The lost violin was clearly still a sore point. He made a show of ignoring Reg's pantomime and shook my hand and hugged and kissed Helen enthusiastically.

'Heh, Helen! I missed you,' said Serge, in French. He hugged her tightly. 'If you ever get fed up with Johnny here give me a ring.'

'I'm fed up with him now,' said Helen. 'What's your number again?'

Serge loved that. He chuckled and then unexpectedly suddenly swung round and play-punched Reg in the stomach. The pair of them grappled together and ended up laughing.

'*Le Pirate*, he's typical *rosbif*,' said Serge. 'Everything's a big joke, eh?'

Reg put his arm round his shoulders. 'Never mind, mate, that violin's bound to turn up one day.' He looked at us... 'Not!'

'Were you at the funeral yesterday, Serge?' asked Helen. 'The one for the couple who got murdered.'

'You're joking, I wouldn't go to their funeral... and they wouldn't come to mine.'

'Didn't you get on with them?' said Helen.

'They were jewellery dealers. Jewellery dealers keep themselves to themselves in case they get rolled. But now there are a lot more tough gangsters about who don't give a shit. Those two disappeared for ages and no one knew where they were. Some people thought they'd pulled off a big deal somewhere and run away to live on an island. But then their bodies were found in the woods, killed and robbed of everything. God knows how long they'd been there.'

'That's terrible,' said Helen.

'That's the risk you take, I'm afraid, when you deal in valuable gear. In fact, Johnny, I was going to ask you a favour today.'

I was about to say 'anything', like a mug, but managed to stop myself.

'I've got some jewellery I want to sell off, rings mainly. Would you take some of my stock and help me get rid of it?'

'We don't really buy jewellery much,' said Helen, giving me a look.

'No, I'm not asking you to buy it. All I want you to do is take a display cabinet and a few rings and bits of jewellery. I'll make it worth your while. Once they're gone that's it for me. I've decided I don't want to die like them. You never know who'll be next. I've only got a few bits and I don't want to take any risks. I've decided I like living too much.'

I looked at Helen. It didn't seem like that much to ask. Just putting out a display cabinet with a few rings and odds and ends of jewellery in it. Where was the harm in that?

Helen nodded to me. 'OK, Serge,' she said. 'We'll do it, but only if you promise me it's all legit, you rogue.'

Serge shrugged. '*Mais oui*, would I lie to you?'

'Yes,' she said.

He pulled a hurt face, and then laughed and squeezed her arm.

As I set up my stand I could tell it was going to be a real scorcher, just like Reg had said. It was early, but you could already feel the power of the sun as it rose above the old medieval city. This was what the weather was usually like at the height of summer down here in the south-west. When we first moved out from England we would flop out on a bed with an electric fan going, unable to move. Now our blood had thinned down and we could carry on more or less as normal. But on our return visits to England in the summer I noticed that when everyone was walking about in shorts and T-shirts and sandals it felt quite chilly to me and I was obliged to don a pullover, jeans and trainers most of the time. Although I was now acclimatised to the heat here I was glad

I had my parasols to protect me from the full force of the sun. Without them I'd have been fried to a frazzle.

I was laying out our stock when I looked across the way and was surprised to see Angelique hefting a parasol out of Serge's white van and positioning it in its stand. I looked around for Bernard but there was no sign of him. Serge climbed out of the back carrying a display cabinet. He came across with it.

'Here's the jewellery,' he said.

'Where's Bernard?' I asked.

'No idea, Johnny.'

'Angelique's on her own, is she?'

'She's helping me out today.' He placed the cabinet on my table and opened it.

'These rings are all gold and marked with a price tag. If you look on the back of the ticket I've written what the precious stones are and the gold marks.'

'That must be nice,' I said.

'What's that?'

'Having Angelique to help you out.'

'Yes, she's a good worker.'

'Pretty too.'

He glanced up. 'She's not just a pretty face. She's a nice person. I don't really like to see the way Bernard treats her.'

'He *is* a bit of a pig,' I said.

'You said it, Johnny... a right pig.'

He busied himself with his rings.

'I'll leave it to you to decide what discounts you give on these. Bear in mind I want to clear the stock but some of this stuff is really nice. Don't go mad on the reductions.'

I looked at the rings. They were big and shiny and that's about all I could say about them. The scrawl on the tags was hard to decipher. I had never sold jewellery and I wasn't sure I was up to this.

Serge thrust something into my hand. 'Here's the key to the cabinet, Johnny. Make sure you keep it locked when you're not serving. Some people have got light fingers.'

I pocketed the key and tried to concentrate.

'One other thing. The customers for rings like these tend to be fat, rich old bags. I'm warning you now, they can be a right pain in the arse, and sometimes it's difficult and they try your patience.'

'I'll remember that,' I said.

'I know you will, Johnny. You're nice to *les clients*. You shouldn't have any problems.'

I wished I felt so confident.

As people started to arrive I noticed we were set up on both sides of a thoroughfare into the market. It was good in a way because people had to push past and this meant they had to look at our stuff. But it worried me that I couldn't keep an eye on the stock at all times. Since we'd been working the markets in France we'd only ever had a couple of small items stolen from our tables. Generally people were honest and you could even leave your stand unattended for short periods without worrying. But now we had jewellery, albeit in a locked cabinet, I didn't feel quite so relaxed. I could see how jewellery dealers kept themselves to themselves. It was certainly more stressful.

Helen worked beside me as the customers poured into the market square. When the initial rush was over I went for a short stroll to check out how the other dealers were doing.

As I passed Serge's stand Angelique was hefting the base of a painted marble-topped dressing table into position. She was wearing a bright summer frock and despite the heat looked fresh and gorgeous. Serge was leaning over his stand reading a paper. On the way back to the van she pinched his bottom. It was intimate, the sort of thing Helen regularly did to me. He smiled but carried on reading his paper.

I realised Angelique was about to try and lift the marble top of the dressing table out of the van on her own and rushed to help her. We carried it over together and set it in place.

She was grateful. 'Thank you so much, er…'

'John,' I said.

'Ah yes, *Jean.*' She pronounced it the French way. 'You're the English *brocanteur* aren't you, Serge's friend?'

'That's right.' I was flattered she remembered me.

'Yes, Serge often talks about you.' She smiled indulgently over to where he was absorbed in his paper. He was oblivious.

'I'd better get back,' I said. 'My wife Helen's manning the stand on her own and it's getting quite busy.'

'That's her over there with the red hair?' she said pointing towards our stand. 'She's nice. I think I've seen her before.'

'Yes, probably,' I said. 'We often work together.'

'It's *agréable, n'est-ce-pas*, to work together, sharing the load,' she said.

I agreed it was. As I was leaving, Serge looked up.

'How's it going, Johnny? Making a fortune?'

I nodded and pulled a face at him and he buried his head back in his paper.

At our stand Helen was in the middle of a rush of buying fever.

'It's gone mad here,' she said, 'I really need a hand. If you can wrap up this dinner service I can see to the rings.'

There was a cluster of older women round Serge's jewellery cabinet. Helen went over to serve them. They appeared to be charmed by her English manner. The rings were selling well because of the discounts, although some of the prices seemed incredibly high even with the reductions. Quite a few were encrusted with diamonds (it said on the tickets) and the women were impressed and keen to pay up for them in cash. We were beginning to see why jewellery dealers did so well. It was a revelation.

Helen went off to prepare lunch and I was left alone coping with the punters, who seemed to be getting less accumulative as thoughts of food filled their minds.

A jolly *gitan* family arrived, pushing their way through. There were numerous wild-faced, laughing children who expressed great interest in the objects on our stand, picking up pieces and demanding to know what they were.

A confident little lad in a blue and white shell suit was fascinated by our wind-up gramophone, delighted by the music it produced when the needle was lowered onto the rotating shellac disc. I had a loud 78 recording of 'The Dam Busters March', which always impressed both kids and grown-ups. I was yet again amused at how a generation of children brought up on computers in the digital age viewed the music produced on a mechanical gramophone as some kind of strange magic.

His sisters were more interested in the teddy bears and dolls, cuddling them, asking if they could take them home. As I chatted to them I was conscious of how Gypsy families like this were regarded by the locals: thieving *gitans*, not to be trusted. But they were charming and I had no intention of being so prejudiced. I realised I was subconsciously making a special effort to empathise with them.

They shouted across to their dad, who was so overweight he was having to use walking sticks to get about. Despite his disability (he was so fat I couldn't imagine him squeezing through a caravan door) he still carried himself with a proud, macho air.

Their mother, a voluptuous blonde, was immediately drawn to Serge's cabinet of jewellery. She was accompanied by a vivacious dark-haired young woman who might have been her sister. They were keen to try on the rings and I was happy to oblige as they flirted outrageously, knowingly flattering my male ego.

They picked out a large diamond ring. The mother slipped it on and commented on the quality of the gold and how the diamond sparkled in the sunlight.

She loved it. She was hooked.

She made me a ridiculously low offer (less than half the ticket price) and I had to explain that I was selling it for a friend and would ask him if he was willing to let it go so cheaply. She gave me a secret smile and said she would be back later with the cash. They all went off noisily together laughing and joking. That was the last I'd see of them, I thought.

It was well and truly past *midi* now, so I covered the tables, locked Serge's jewellery cabinet in the back of the van and headed for where our caravan was parked in the shade under the trees.

A delicious smoky smell of barbecued burgers greeted me. Reg was cooking them over a portable charcoal grill, dressed in shorts and sandals and wearing a stripy apron.

'Fancy a burger, mate? I've got plenty.'

'Ta, mate, but I'm vegetarian,' I said, feeling slightly embarrassed to be so finicky.

'Oh right, veggie is it?' he said, like he expected as much.

Rita was lying back on a plastic lounger in a bikini outside the caravan swigging from a bottle with a fag in her hand. When she saw me she waved and took a deep drag.

'How's it going, lovey? Making a lot of money?'

I told Reg about the *gitan* family and their interest in the rings.

'Bloody 'ell, mate! Don't let bloody gypos try on jewellery. Are you soft or what?'

'They seemed friendly enough,' I said. 'They wanted to buy a diamond ring but I don't think they could afford it.'

'Afford it? Course they can afford it! But pikeys like that don't buy valuables, they nick 'em. If they come sniffing round my stuff I tell 'em "*Dégagez!*", which is like sod off in froggy. That gets rid of 'em.'

'I don't think they were that bad,' I said.

'Look, John, I live with gypos. I buy off 'em, stay on their caravan sites. Take my word for it. Don't trust 'em. They're outside our society. They live off their wits. If you give 'em an inch they take a mile. Once they suss you as a mug you've 'ad it.'

I couldn't help feeling he was being predictably prejudiced. I believed if you treated people with respect then they would appreciate it and act accordingly and return the favour.

Helen had been chatting to Angelique and had invited her and Serge to join us for lunch. When they arrived we all sat down together.

Rita fussed over Serge, despite Angelique being there.

''Ere you are darling, want a burger?' She appeared to have developed a permanent soft spot for him.

When I told him how the jewellery was going he was pleased. 'That's it, Johnny, let's get rid of it, eh? I'm selling off a lot of my other baubles.'

'Tell him about the gypos,' said Reg. 'He loves gypos after all that violin business.' He gave Serge a nudge. 'That's right, ain't it, Sergie? You love the old *gitans*, don't you?' He went through his violin mime again.

Serge looked at me, questioningly. When I explained about the Gypsy family, I was surprised by his reaction. 'If they want to buy, go ahead, Johnny... But be careful. I don't need to tell you that.'

The afternoon was baking hot and the square had emptied. The air was shimmering in the heat and I dozed off sitting in a camping chair in the shade. I woke up later feeling groggy, like I might have got a touch of the sun. But despite the heat the afternoon buyers were beginning to drift back. I had to get out there. Helen stayed in the caravan. She could take less heat than me, and she, Rita and Angelique were having a chat and a laugh, no doubt at the expense of us men.

I uncovered our tables and was replacing Serge's jewellery cabinet when the blonde woman reappeared with her raven-haired friend. Could she have another look at that ring? And had I asked my friend about lowering the price?

I unlocked the cabinet and passed her the ring. She tried it on again and her friend went through the others, trying to find one that took her fancy.

As I served them I felt a hand on my arm and turned to be confronted by a diminutive Indian couple – a neat little man in a dark suit, white shirt and tie, and a woman wearing a colourful silk sari. I was taken aback, as I had never seen an Indian couple like this in this country region of France. He was charming and well spoken. I was completely disarmed.

They decided on an inexpensive ring almost immediately and he passed over a five-hundred-euro note to pay for it. I have heard these purple euro notes referred to colloquially as Bin Ladens – 'everyone's always looking for them but they are hardly ever seen'. It was normally only the Spanish who carried such large denomination notes. They liked to pay in cash and someone had told me it was because they had a huge 'black' economy and mistrusted banks.

I was trying to keep an eye on all my customers at once but it wasn't so easy on my own without Helen to help me.

I had opened my bumbag, searching through for change, when the charming Indian woman reached over and started flicking her fingers through the notes in my bag, pointing out how much I should give her husband.

My instinctive reaction was to pull away.

'*Excusez-moi, madame!*' I exclaimed, alarmed, jumping back.

'I've changed my mind,' said the little man, seemingly offended.

He passed back the ring.

I was thrown by this sudden change of behaviour. But the customer is always right, I thought grudgingly to myself, the customer is always right.

'*Bien sûr, m'sieu, sans problème.*'

I handed him back his bloody 'Bin Laden'. They were a flipping nuisance anyway, as no French shopkeepers would take them.

I looked around, feeling put out and befuddled by what had happened.

The blonde Gypsy woman and her friend had vanished. And when I turned back, the Indian couple had also disappeared, melting into the crowd.

But then I spotted them on the far side of the square. They appeared to be talking to the big fat Gypsy I had seen earlier.

Instinctively I checked Serge's jewellery cabinet. The diamond ring had gone and several others seemed to be missing as well. A feeling of panic and disbelief overtook me. I left my stand and ran over to where I had seen the Indian couple and the fat Gypsy. But there was no sign of them.

It dawned on me that I'd been taken for a mug in a professionally executed 'sting'.

I felt so stupid. How could I tell Serge what a total twat I'd been... robbed in broad daylight right under my nose? The Gypsies and the Indian couple had been working as a team. I'd been set up.

What an idiot!

When I told Helen she was shocked and blamed herself for not coming to help. 'What the hell's Serge going to say?'

I left her on the stand and went over sheepishly to tell him.

He listened as I told him what had happened. His eyes widened in disbelief. When I had finished he looked at me sternly.

'Well, that's my retirement ruined. He put his head in his hands. I watched him and felt like a shit. He suddenly spluttered and burst out laughing, slapping me on the back.

'Heh, Johnny, I'd like to say I'm upset, but it's really quite a funny story, I'm sorry. Look it's my own fault, I should have warned you that gold attracts *gitans* like flies and never ever let them touch the goods. It's asking for trouble. And don't feel too bad, none of the stones in those rings were actually diamonds. Most of them are semi-precious or worthless cut glass.'

The relief I felt when he told me this was spectacular. But when I realised he'd had us unwittingly offering fake diamond rings as genuine to the public I felt totally used.

'You mean to tell me most of those rings are virtually worthless?'

'Not worthless exactly, Johnny. Let's just say they've got a high mark up.'

'Oh great! So I had once again been acting as an innocent accomplice in another of Serge's little rip-off schemes. Helen was right. Nothing Serge did was legit.

On the other hand the blonde Gypsy woman and the Indian couple had been to a lot of trouble for very little. That was some consolation, but despite it all I couldn't help feeling a grudging respect for the way they'd pulled it off. I was impressed how these diverse members of two marginalised sections of society had worked successfully together. There were lessons there for us all. If we could work together in harmony as these Gypsies and Asians had then the world might be a better place. Maybe not if our joint efforts were used for swindling people, though.

The heat was blistering as the afternoon wore on and we huddled under our parasols, unable to move. It was so hot that the market square was virtually deserted. I was fetching Helen a cold drink from the caravan when I passed Reg and Rita laid out under their caravan awning. They appeared to have given up.

'Blimey, it must be forty degrees,' said Reg. 'Might as well pack up. Punters don't come out in heat like this.'

I reluctantly told him what had happened, how I'd been conned by the blonde Gypsy woman and an Indian couple.

'Didn't I warn you about the gypos?' he said. 'I don't like to say this, but dear oh dear, what a sucker!' Good job it was only Serge's tat that got nicked.' He laughed.

'But an Indian couple, that's unusual round here,' he said.

I didn't like to tell him I harboured a grudging admiration for the way they'd carried out the 'sting'. And I certainly couldn't accept his blanket condemnation of a whole race of people, despite what had happened.

'They must have come from that big gypo encampment on the edge of town,' he said. 'We could go up there later and look for the perpetrators. That fat bloke'd be easy to spot for a start. I could swipe him round the back of the head with a length of four-by-two, knock the fat bugger out. Teach him a lesson, that would.'

'What about the gendarmes?' said Rita.

'I think it might be best to leave well alone,' I said. 'It would be hard to prove and I haven't got any witnesses. And anyway I don't think Serge would want me to draw police attention to his jewellery sales.'

'It's rotten though,' said Rita, 'having his stuff nicked. That poor little Bastarde bloke.'

'Serge,' I said.

'Yeah, that poor little Serge Bastarde bloke... he doesn't seem to be having much luck lately, does he?'

'I wouldn't waste too much sympathy on him,' I said. 'He wasn't that worried. He said the rings weren't worth much anyway. I don't think they were even gold and they certainly weren't real diamonds.'

'Yeah, anything bright and glittery sends the gypos mad,' said Reg. 'They pretend they know all about it, like they do with violins, but mostly they're just bluffing.'

I was going to point out that they knew exactly what they were doing when they lifted Serge's Stradivarius, but decided to let it pass.

By early evening most of the *brocanteurs* had packed up and covered their stands. The weather forecast was good for the second day of the fair so the majority of dealers had left their parasols up, confident there would be no unexpected storm during the night.

I went over to see Serge who was hammering guy ropes into the ground just in case. Angelique was helping him, holding the pegs, leaning back, closing her eyes as Serge wielded the mallet.

I waited till they'd finished, then passed over the takings from the jewellery sales. It came to a considerable sum and after my experience during the day I wasn't keen to have it in the caravan overnight.

'I'd rather you kept it in the van, Serge. It'll be safer,' I said.

'OK, Johnny. But I'm not sleeping in the van tonight. I've booked into a hotel in the town. Can't have Angelique all humped up in the van can we? I'm taking her out for a meal. She deserves it.'

Angelique gave me a shy smile.

She had changed yet again. She was now dressed in a slinky red number and wearing her trademark black lacy stockings with white high heels. She looked stunning. And Serge had a look on his face like the cat that got the cream.

'Well, have a nice evening,' I said, giving him a knowing smile.

'Thanks, Johnny. We will.' Angelique took hold of his arm and he half-turned, gave me a secret wink and they walked off into the sunset.

20

HANDBAGS AND WARRIORS

I headed back to our caravan, chuckling to myself. I couldn't wait to tell Helen the news about Serge and Angelique, how they now appeared to be an item. How had Serge managed it? How had he managed to pull a woman like her? It was astonishing. What a turn up!

When I told Helen she was gleeful. 'I've been bursting to tell you. Angelique told us all about it at lunch. We three women had long chats in the caravan after you men had gone.'

'You mean you knew and didn't say anything?'

'I kept meaning to tell you but we were so busy and with all that business with the rings, I never got a chance.'

There was me, a bloke, thinking he'd managed to glean a juicy bit of gossip to pass on, only to discover his wife already knew all about it and in every detail.

'What did she say then?'

'Well, she kept on about how funny and handsome Serge was and how she loved being with him and asking us if we thought he was too. I couldn't believe it. I think he's pretty much physically repulsive but Rita seems to have a soft spot for him.'

'Blimey! So what's his secret then? It's not to do with size or anything like that?' I said, trying not to express a prurient interest.

'Well…'

'It is to do with size?' I spluttered. 'It's got to be.'

Helen laughed out loud. She was winding me up.

'No, we didn't talk about that… strangely enough.'

'Well, what about Bernard, does he know about it?'

'Not yet. But she's going to dump him.'

'She said that?'

'Yes, and that's not all.'

'There's more?'

'Listen to this… Serge has decided to give up *brocante*, she's pregnant and they're going to get married and move to Martinique.'

'No!'

'Yes, apparently it's been going on for a while. She says she loves him, they were made for each other and she wishes she'd met him years ago. She says Serge told her he's got a small fortune tucked away and with his retirement money he need never work again.'

I was speechless. There was no fathoming the ways of women. And I wasn't sure about Serge's secret fortune. It sounded like he was shooting her a line.

The evening gradually cooled as we sat outside our caravan under the stars, watching the reflected lights shimmering on the River Tarn. I could smell the river snaking its way through the town. It carried the scent of maize fields, the open countryside and hot balmy summer nights. At least I imagined it did.

We could see the tip of Rita's fag glowing in the gloom across the way and the dying embers of Reg's barbecue grill as a bright full moon rose in the sky. There was a crunch on the gravel and Reg appeared.

''Ere, Rita told me all about Serge and that Angelique sort.' He was jubilant. 'Who'd 'ave thought it, eh? A cracking bird like that falling for a funny little geezer like 'im. Talk about Beauty and the Beast... or Snow White and the Seven Dwarfs in his case.'

'I know,' I said. 'Brilliant, isn't it?'

'Well good luck to the little blokey,' said Reg. 'I know I wouldn't turn her down...' He glanced over at Rita's fag glow. '... if I was 'im.'

'They must see something in him,' I said. 'Women, you know.'

'I suppose,' said Reg. 'I wonder what it is.'

'Well, she thinks he's funny and handsome so that's all that matters,' said Helen.

'He's knocked her up though hasn't he?' said Reg. 'Oo-er! The dirty little rascal.' He let out a delighted cackle. 'Let's hope the kiddie looks more like her than him.'

'Oh, he's not that bad,' said Helen. She's changed her tune, I thought to myself, after saying he was physically repulsive.

'Anyway, we're turning in,' said Reg. 'Tomorrow's another day and all that. Night, all.' He crunched off back to his caravan and we heard Rita scream and give a little giggle.

Helen and I were in bed together in the caravan.

'It's funny,' I said, 'I was just thinking about Serge and how everyone advised me to steer clear of him because he's a load of trouble. And now he's getting married and swanning off to live in another country I'm going to miss him.'

'Are you mad?' said Helen, 'He's completely incorrigible – passing all that fake jewellery on us, getting you into scrapes and trouble. I thought it was all going to end in tears. He's got the luck of the devil and so have you. You two are a right pair. Tweedledum and Tweedledee!'

There was no answer to that.

'Still, at least Angelique loves him,' said Helen.

I felt myself nodding off to the sounds of the night – an owl hooting and another responding in the distance; a dog barking, setting off an answering chorus across town.

I was awake in a flash. Someone was screaming.

'What the hell's that?'

'I heard that too,' whispered Helen. 'Is that Rita?'

There was a loud crash... footsteps running on the gravel.

'Stay there. I'm going to have a look.' I opened the caravan door, grabbing the lump hammer I kept handy just in case.

Helen was right behind me.

There was a blood-curdling howl.

We looked out onto the square. Someone was heading for the trees... followed closely by a stark-naked white body luminescent in the moonlight, long hair flying, yelling a war cry, brandishing a length of two-by-four – Reg!

Rita was at the caravan door, ashen faced.

We went over to her.

'A hand...' said Rita. She was on the edge, holding back hysteria.

'A hand... reached in through the window... nicked me handbag.

We could hear Reg's voice in the distance yelling, the squeal of tyres – a car accelerating away.

'Oh Christ!' shrieked Rita. 'My Reggie!'

Everything went quiet.

'Hang on. I'm going after them,' I said, tightening my grip on my lump hammer.

'No wait,' said Helen. 'Someone's coming.'

We stood peering into the darkness, nerves on edge.

A figure materialised out of the shadows: a naked Stone Age warrior. It was Reg, length of two-by-four in one hand, handbag in the other.

'Oi-oi,' he said. 'Nearly got the bastard!'

Rita ran to him and put her arms round him.

'Are you OK? Did you see who it was?' asked Helen, averting her eyes.

'Dunno,' said Reg. 'But I don't think they'll be back tonight.'

'You got the handbag back then?' I said. Like Helen I was concentrating on his face, trying not to let my eyes slip.

'Yeah, the bloke took one look at me behind him and chucked it. He was lucky; if I'd 'ave caught him, I'd 'ave killed 'im. There was a getaway car waiting to pick him up and he got away... worse luck.'

He slung down his piece of two-by-four.

'Maybe now we can get some kip.'

Helen and I said our goodnights and hurried back to our caravan. The moment we got inside we both collapsed with laughter.

'I know that was awful but the sight of Reg!' said Helen.

'They picked on the wrong bloke there,' I said. 'He's a maniac.'

We tried to get back to sleep but it was hard. One of us would snigger and set the other one off. Eventually I drifted off with the image of the naked Reg burned on my memory.

21

INTO THE WILD BLUE YONDER

'Martinique is a beautiful island. Did you know it's part of the European Union and its currency is the euro? Imagine that, Johnny – nowhere near Europe, in the Caribbean, and you don't need to change your money. Marvellous! And they speak French there – another bonus.'

We were waiting at Bordeaux airport and Serge was waxing lyrical about his prospective new home.

'So you'll be off on one of your little *expéditions* then, soon after you get there?'

'Heh, no, Johnny. I'm finished with all that. I'm retiring and looking after my new family.' He gazed fondly at Angelique, who despite being six months pregnant was dressed immaculately in a stylish designer number. 'Besides, it wouldn't be the same without my *rosbif* sidekick, would it?'

Helen raised her eyes to heaven. 'Yes, well, he's had enough of being led astray by you Mr Bastarde, thanks very much.'

I grinned sheepishly at Serge. I was feeling a mixture of relief that I wouldn't be mixed up in his future schemes and regret for the fact that life might be less interesting without him. It was true he had led me astray but I had learned a lot along the way.

'She calls us Tweedledum and Tweedledee,' I said.

'What is this Tweedledum and Tweedledee?' asked Angelique.

'They were a pair of twins in *Alice in Wonderland*,' I said.' 'You know the book by Lewis Carroll? A couple of bozos.'

She looked blank.

'I'm not sure he's an author who's very well known in France,' I said.

Serge looked anxious. 'I hope Robespierre will be all right. I hate to think of him freighted up in that plastic cage.'

'He'll be fine,' I said reassuringly. 'They're used to transporting pets.' I'd have felt the same and tried not to think about Robespierre lonely in his box.

Now the moment had come for them to leave I had a lump in my throat. It had all happened so quickly. I was going to miss him. Helen and Angelique had become friends. They both shared an interest in antiques and had taken to having long chats on the phone, no doubt discussing their relationships, too. Serge and Angelique were off making a new start but we were going to have to carry on earning a living on the markets in France. I had no pension or nest egg to fall back on like Serge. Maybe I would one day come across that legendary antique find that would earn me a fortune and set me up for the rest of my life. But I wasn't holding my breath.

'You'll come and stay with us though, won't you?' said Angelique.

'Of course we will,' said Helen. 'Try and stop us. Martinique sounds fantastic. We'll keep in touch anyway… don't forget to email and phone.'

The indicator board was flashing that their flight was boarding.

Serge took me aside. He slipped something into my hand. It was a key with an address on a label. 'Listen, Johnny, don't say anything but I want you to go and collect some stuff from this address and put it in my garage.'

I couldn't believe he was asking me this. 'No, I'm not doing any of that any more. You're supposed to be starting a new life, what's the matter with you?'

'Oh, all right. You're probably right, Johnny. Have this anyway.'

'What is it?'

'It's a present… for you.'

I recognised it. It was a leather-bound book – Marcel's *L'Art de Péter*.

'I couldn't,' I said.

'No, I want you to have it, Johnny. You helped me. I was going to sell it but somehow it didn't feel right.'

'Thanks,' I said. 'I'll treasure it always.'

'You can sell it,' he said, 'if you need the money.'

'I'll try not to,' I said, thinking how it was purportedly worth a three-month holiday lying on soft sandy beaches sipping exotic cocktails surrounded by beautiful women.

Helen waved to us to hurry up. 'Come on, they'll miss their flight.'

We watched them through security. They turned, waved and disappeared through customs.

I was holding Serge's present with a tear in my eye.

Helen took my arm. 'Come on, dear,' she gave me a big hug. 'Now, be honest, how long do you think they'll stay out there?'

I thought for a bit. 'About five weeks.'

'Oh, that long?' she said.

Other titles available from Summersdale

A Chateau Of One's Own

Restoration Misadventures in France

SAM JUNEAU

A CHATEAU OF ONE'S OWN
Restoration Misadventures in France

Sam Juneau

ISBN: 978-1-84024-641-4   Paperback   £7.99

Sam and Bud were ordinary first-time homebuyers in their early thirties. Their intention in moving to France was to create a simple life and spend more time with their children. The home they actually bought was an impressive seventeenth-century chateau in the Loire valley with over thirty rooms, 156 windows and 40 acres of land.

With only modest savings, the couple launched the challenging project of restoring this crumbling monster of a building to its former glory and opening a bed and breakfast in the process. This is the hilarious story of behind the scenes at a B&B that required constant disaster relief: think *Fawlty Towers* in an extraordinary setting.

'*the perfect read for anyone considering a grandiose home makeover project and for all of us who dream of a life in France*'
LIVING FRANCE magazine

'*an amazing journey*'   LIVING ABROAD magazine

'*Hilarious... Engaging tale... A refreshing warts-and-all account of what follows that impulsive buy*'
SCOTTISH SUNDAY EXPRESS

Richard Wiles

Bon Courage!

A French renovation in rural Limousin

BON COURAGE!

A French renovation in rural Limousin

Richard Wiles

ISBN: 978-1-84024-360-4   Paperback   £8.99

A dilapidated, rat-infested stone barn set amidst thirteen acres of unkempt pasture and overgrown woodland might not be many people's vision of a potential dream home. But for Englishman Richard and his wife Al, the cavernous, oak-beamed building in a sleepy hamlet in the Limousin region of France is perfect.

Tussles with French bureaucracy allied with fierce storms that wreak havoc on the property do little to dampen their resolve as they immerse themselves in the *calme* of this quiet corner of France, dreaming of taking trips in Richard's hot-air balloon and starting their very own llama farm.

The couple's colourful, often eccentric neighbours watch their progress with curiosity: the jovial ex-gendarme and his wife, who seems able to foretell the weather; the lonely widow who offers copious amounts of *gâteau* in exchange for convivial chat; and the brawny cattleman with suspicious motives for cleaning up the couple's land.

Told by a well-intentioned if often hapless do-it-yourselfer, Richard's hilarious and heartwarming tale of a new life in France resounds to the Gallic refrain, '*Bon courage!*'

'*This book will trigger dreams...*'

COUNTRY HOUSE & HOME

Richard Wiles

Bonne Chance!

Building a Life in Rural France

BONNE CHANCE!
Building a Life in Rural France

Richard Wiles

ISBN: 978-1-84024-493-9   Paperback   £7.99

Deep in the Limousin countryside, Richard Wiles bought his dream home. But little did he expect to be living full time in the dilapidated farmhouse and struggling to finish the conversion during the insect plagues of summer and the harsh blizzards of winter.

Watched by his bemused neighbours, Richard pursued his more unusual dreams of raising llamas, hot-air ballooning and marathon running whilst trying to keep the roof over his head. Told with unfailing humour and optimism, this is a unique tale of overcoming the challenges of building a home, and a life, in France.

'...*lifts the lid on the reality of building a home and a life in France*'   A PLACE IN THE SUN magazine

'*I would certainly recommend it to anyone as holiday reading, to anyone visiting or contemplating living in France and to all aspiring llama keepers, hot-air balloonists and marathon runners*'
                                    DESTINATION FRANCE

TOUT SWEET

Hanging up my High Heels for a New Life in France

Karen Wheeler

ISBN: 978-1-84024-761-9   Paperback   £7.99

In her mid-thirties, fashion editor Karen has it all: a handsome boyfriend, a fab flat in west London and an array of gorgeous shoes. But when Eric leaves, she hangs up her Manolos and waves goodbye to her glamorous city lifestyle to go it alone in a run-down house in rural Poitou-Charentes, central western France.

Acquiring a host of new friends and unsuitable suitors, she learns that true happiness can be found in the simplest of things – a bike ride through the countryside on a summer evening, or a kir or three in a neighbour's courtyard.

Perfect summer reading for anyone who dreams of chucking away their BlackBerry in favour of real blackberrying and downshifting to France.

'an hilarious account of a fashion guru who swaps Prada for paintbrushes and Pineau in rural France'
                                              MAIL ON SUNDAY Travel

Have you enjoyed this book?
If so, why not write a review
on your favourite website?

Thanks very much for buying
this Summersdale book.

www.summersdale.com